4/03

THE VIETNAM WAR

**GREAT
SPEECHES
IN
HISTORY**

Ryn Shane-Armstrong
and Lynn Armstrong,
Book Editors

Daniel Leone, *President*

Bonnie Szumski, *Publisher*

Scott Barbour, *Managing Editor*

GREENHAVEN
PRESS®

THOMSON

———✳———™

GALE

San Diego • Detroit • New York • San Francisco • Cleveland
New Haven, Conn. • Waterville, Maine • London • Munich

THOMSON
GALE

This book is dedicated to Scott Armstrong:
brother, uncle, Vietnam War veteran.

For more information, contact
Greenhaven Press
27500 Drake Rd.
Farmington Hills, MI 48331-3535
Or you can visit our Internet site at http://www.gale.com

Cover credit: Associated Press
National Archives, 18, 41, 71, 82, 99, 170

LIBRARY OF CONGRESS CATALOGING-IN-PUBLICATION DATA
The Vietnam War / Ryn Shane-Armstrong and Lynn Armstrong, book editors.
p. cm. — (Greenhaven Press's great speeches in history)
Includes bibliographical references and index.
ISBN 0-7377-1434-4 (pbk. : alk. paper) — ISBN 0-7377-1433-6 (lib. : alk. paper)
1. Vietnamese Conflict, 1961–1975—Sources. I. Shane-Armstrong, Ryn, and Armstrong, Lynn. II. Great speeches in history series.
DS556.2 .V56 2003
959.704'32—dc21   2002027890

Contents

Chapter 1: Prewar Diplomacy

   The French imperialists abused their own standards
   of liberty, equality, and fraternity by denying democratic freedom to the Vietnamese people. The Democratic Republic of Vietnam is now a free and independent country.

   Acts of aggression against free peoples anywhere
   threatens America. U.S. policy will be to support
   countries anywhere in the world that are resisting
   attempted subjugation by armed minoritics or by
   outside pressures.

   The United States should strongly resist the attempt
   by Chinese and Soviet Communists to subvert a
   democratic South Vietnam.

   Military intervention by the United States in support
   of the French is futile without the support of the
   Vietnamese people.

Chapter 2: American Intervention

Chapter 3: The War Abroad

the Unknown Soldier of the Vietnam War, the
United States finally honors Vietnam War veterans,
but the war has not ended for the families of missing soldiers.

Foreword

I have a dream that one day this nation will rise up and live out the true meaning of its creed: "We hold these truths to be self-evident: that all men are created equal."

I have a dream that one day on the red hills of Georgia the sons of former slaves and the sons of former slave owners will be able to sit down together at the table of brotherhood.

I have a dream that one day even the state of Mississippi, a state sweltering with the heat of injustice, sweltering with the heat of oppression, will be transformed into an oasis of freedom and justice.

I have a dream that my four little children will one day live in a nation where they will not be judged by the color of their skin but by the content of their character.

Perhaps no speech in American history resonates as deeply as Martin Luther King Jr.'s "I Have a Dream," delivered in 1963 before a rapt audience of 250,000 on the steps of the Lincoln Memorial in Washington, D.C. Decades later, the speech still enthralls those who read or hear it, and stands as a philosophical guidepost for contemporary discourse on racism.

What distinguishes "I Have a Dream" from the hundreds of other speeches given during the civil rights era are King's eloquence, lyricism, and use of vivid metaphors to convey abstract ideas. Moreover, "I Have a Dream" serves not only as a record of history—a testimony to the racism that permeated American society during the 1960s—but it is also a historical event in its own right. King's speech, aired live on national television, marked the first time that the grave injustice of racism was fully articulated to a mass audience in a way that was both logical and evocative. Julian Bond, a fellow participant in the civil rights movement and student of King's, states that

> King's dramatic 1963 "I Have a Dream" speech before the Lincoln Memorial cemented his place as first among equals in civil rights leadership; from this first televised mass meeting, an American audience saw and heard the unedited oratory of America's finest preacher, and for the first time, a mass white audience heard the undeniable justice of black demands.

Moreover, by helping people to understand the justice of the civil rights movement's demands, King's speech helped to transform the nation. In 1964, a year after the speech was delivered, President Lyndon B. Johnson signed the Civil Rights Act, which outlawed segregation in public facilities and discrimination in employment. In 1965, Congress passed the Voting Rights Act, which forbids restrictions, such as literacy tests, that were commonly used in the South to prevent blacks from voting. King's impact on the country's laws illustrates the power of speech to bring about real change.

Greenhaven Press's Great Speeches in History series offers students an opportunity to read and study some of the greatest speeches ever delivered before an audience. Each volume traces a specific historical era, event, or theme through speeches—both famous and lesser known. An introductory essay sets the stage by presenting background and context. Then a collection of speeches follows, grouped in chapters based on chronology or theme. Each selection is preceded by a brief introduction that offers historical context, biographical information about the speaker, and analysis of the speech. A comprehensive index and an annotated table of contents help readers quickly locate material of interest, and a bibliography serves as a launching point for further research. Finally, an appendix of author biographies provides detailed background on each speaker's life and work. Taken together, the volumes in the Greenhaven Great Speeches in History series offer students vibrant illustrations of history and demonstrate the potency of the spoken word. By reading speeches in their historical context, students will be transported back in time and gain a deeper understanding of the issues that confronted people of the past.

Introduction

"All men are created equal. They are endowed by their Creator with certain inalienable rights; among these are life, liberty, and the pursuit of happiness." These words, which Thomas Jefferson wrote into the U.S. Declaration of Independence, have been an eloquent and fundamental expression of principles central to American democracy since their original expression in Philadelphia in July 1776. Nevertheless, these words, when spoken by a small white-haired Vietnamese man nearly two hundred years later in a tiny country on the other side of the globe, began a conflict in Southeast Asia that became America's longest and most divisive war, a war fought on two fronts: in the jungles of Vietnam and within the American conscience. It was a war that divided the people of the United States more than any issue since the Civil War, a war that affected American politics into the twenty-first century, a war known to the Vietnamese people as the American War and to the American people as the Vietnam War.

He Who Enlightens

The history of Vietnam is a history of colonization by foreign powers. Starting around 1858, French missionaries began colonizing Vietnam; before the end of the century they had consolidated Vietnam, Laos, and Cambodia into a territory that became known as French Indochina. French colonial administrators ruled Indochina, easily suppressing the infrequent revolts of the Vietnamese people for nearly a century, until Vietnamese leader Ho Chi Minh came home.

The man who became known as Ho Chi Minh, meaning "He Who Enlightens," was born Nguyen That Thanh in 1890 in a small village in central Vietnam. The son of a traveling teacher and medicine man, Ho lived under French colonial rule until the age of twenty-one when he left Vietnam on a French ocean freighter to spend most of the next three decades traveling the world under various assumed names.

Ho informally studied political and economic systems as a

worker in many countries, including the United States, where he labored as a construction worker in New York City. He received a more formal education in France and in the USSR, where he learned about Marxism and communism. Relentlessly pursuing independence for his homeland, he presented a petition for Vietnamese independence to the Versailles Peace Conference after World War I; the conference quickly dismissed it. In 1930 Ho founded the Indochinese Communist Party in unsuccessful opposition to French colonial rule.

When Japan occupied Indochina during World War II, Ho Chi Minh, already fifty years old, returned to Vietnam in the hopes of freeing the Vietnamese people from both the Japanese and the French. In 1941 "Uncle Ho" soon created the League for Vietnamese Independence, also known as the Vietminh, and allied his soldiers with American forces to fight the Japanese in Southeast Asia.

In August 1945, at the end of World War II, Ho Chi Minh led the August Revolution, defeating the puppet regime of Emperor Bao Dai, which had been supported by both the French and the Japanese. On September 2, 1945, he declared Vietnamese independence, creating the Democratic Republic of Vietnam. In a show of support, American soldiers stood onstage with Ho Chi Minh as he delivered his Declaration of Independence, quoting from the U.S. Declaration of Independence. During the remainder of 1945 and into 1946, he wrote a series of letters to U.S. president Harry S. Truman in which he reminded Truman of the Vietminh support for American forces in Southeast Asia and expressed his expectation that the United States would support Vietnamese independence against French colonial claims. However, due to his fear that Vietnam would fall under Communist influence, Truman ignored Ho Chi Minh's appeals and refused to support Vietnamese independence.

The Cold War and the Truman Doctrine

President Truman's response to Ho Chi Minh resulted from the global political tensions of the postwar world. After Truman dropped atomic bombs on Japan, effectively ending World War II, the United States and the Western European nations reluctantly prepared for a new kind of world conflict. The presence of atomic weapons required limited warfare in future international conflicts in order to avoid nuclear catastrophe, yet the postwar rise of nationalism increased international tensions as indigenous peoples ended centuries of colonial rule by overthrowing European imperial powers. As these countries chose new economic and political systems, an ideological battle developed between the competing systems of capitalism and communism. The resulting political and military rivalry became known as the Cold War.

U.S. policy makers had been debating foreign policy strategies concerning nationalism and communism since before World War II. During the war, the State Department under President Franklin Roosevelt considered two postwar strategies for French Indochina. The European Desk, concerned with U.S. relations with European countries, recommended a security alliance with France against communism and the reestablishment of French colonial control in Indochina. The Far East Desk, concerned with U.S. relations with Asian countries, suggested that world stability would require supporting anticolonial forces in Southeast Asia. They quoted President Roosevelt, who had said, "dynamic forces leading toward self-government are growing in Asia; that the United States, as a great democracy, cannot and must not try to retard this development." Before his death in 1945, Roosevelt expressed his support for self-determination in Indochina. Nevertheless, after Roosevelt's death, President Truman adopted the European Desk's policy of alliance with European imperial powers to contain the spread of communism. Therefore, fearing Ho Chi Minh's Communist background, Truman ignored Ho's appeals for recognition and supported French colonial claims in Vietnam instead.

In March 1947, reacting to Communist aggression in Greece and Turkey, Truman declared his policy for containing communism, which, known as the Truman Doctrine, would become the justification for American intervention in Vietnam. In an address to Congress, he condemned Communist states as "totalitarian regimes" and pledged American resistance to Communist aggression worldwide and American support for "free peoples everywhere."

The First Vietnam War and the Geneva Accords

In 1946 French forces began a war to retake Indochina from the Vietminh guerrillas. President Truman authorized $15 million in military aid to the French in 1950, beginning American involvement in Vietnam; the United States contributed $3 billion and 80 percent of French war supplies during the next four years. After Truman refused his appeals, Ho Chi Minh appealed to Communist China for help, and China began sending weapons and military advisers to the Vietminh. General Vo Nguyen Giap soon transformed his guerrilla fighters into a modern army, and after a determined two-month siege of Dien Bien Phu in northern Vietnam, Giap and his soldiers defeated the French forces on May 7, 1954.

On May 8, 1954, representatives from France and Vietnam met in Geneva, Switzerland, to discuss a cease-fire. After weeks of intense debate, peace negotiators came to an agreement in June. The Geneva Accords consisted of three major stipulations: The French colonists would leave Vietnam; Vietnam would be split along the seventeenth parallel between Communist North Vietnam and democratic South Vietnam; and free elections would be held within two years to determine the leadership of a unified Vietnam.

One month prior to the meeting in Geneva, during a press conference on April 7, 1954, U.S. president Dwight D. Eisenhower had explained his "domino theory" of foreign relations. Eisenhower suggested that each country that fell to communism would make it easier for the next country to fall, like a row of toppling dominoes. U.S. foreign policy advisers expected that free elections would elect the popular Ho Chi Minh, bringing Vietnam under Communist control and beginning the Communist domination of Asian nations. American representatives therefore refused to sign the agreement. Instead, Secretary of State John Foster Dulles organized the Southeast Asia Treaty Organization, an alliance of the eight nations of Australia, France, Great Britain, New Zealand, Pakistan, the Philippines, Thailand, and the United States, to resist Communist aggression in Southeast Asia.

The Diem Regime

In October 1955 South Vietnamese president Ngo Dinh Diem, with U.S. encouragement, refused to hold reunification elections. Instead, Diem held his own elections in South Vietnam; when he won, he declared the independence of South Vietnam, renaming it the Republic of Vietnam (RVN). Due to his strong anti-Communist stance, the United States supported Diem and, in violation of the Geneva Accords, U.S. presidents Eisenhower and Kennedy sent aid to South Vietnam, including financial aid, American engineers to repair a crumbling infrastructure, and military advisers to train the Army of the Republic of Vietnam.

Diem was hated by many of his people and deemed untrustworthy by most, including many of his American supporters. A wealthy Catholic in a country of poor Buddhists and more an outsider than a representative of his people, Diem became increasingly repressive. Attempting to limit Vietminh influence, Diem's secret police tortured and killed thousands of Vietnamese people, including peaceful Buddhist monks, causing many Vietnamese to turn to the Communists for help. In 1960 South Vietnamese rebels formed the National Liberation Front (NLF) and began guerrilla warfare against Diem. The Vietminh supported the NLF rebels, called Vietcong by Diem, with military intelligence and weaponry.

On November 2, 1963, with the implicit support of President John F. Kennedy and Ambassador Henry Cabot Lodge, Diem was assassinated and his government overthrown by a military coup. During the next two years, ten different regimes ruled an unstable South Vietnam, and Vietcong influence grew to include nearly 75 percent of the South Vietnamese population.

The Gulf of Tonkin Resolution

President Dwight D. Eisenhower had begun sending military advisers to South Vietnam, and President John F. Kennedy continued the policy, increasing the number of advisers from nine hundred to more than sixteen thousand before his assassination on November 22, 1963. Two days after Kennedy's

death, President Lyndon B. Johnson announced his continuing support for the South Vietnamese government and, during
Johnson's administration, the number of military advisers
steadily increased to more than twenty-seven thousand by
mid-1964.

On August 2, 1964, North Vietnamese patrol boats attacked the USS *Maddox* in the Gulf of Tonkin off the eastern
shore of North Vietnam. Although shocked and angered by
the attacks, President Johnson and his advisers had decided
to respond only with an angry letter when another attack
was reported on August 4.

Three days later, the almost unanimous passage of the
Southeast Asia Resolution by both houses of the U.S. Congress gave Johnson the power to use "all necessary steps, including the use of armed force" in Southeast Asia. Only two
senators voted against the resolution: Ernest Gruening and
Wayne Morse. These senators contended that the Gulf of
Tonkin events were North Vietnamese defensive measures
provoked by American support of secret maritime operations
against the North Vietnamese.

Operation Rolling Thunder and American Intervention

In February 1965 President Johnson authorized Operation
Rolling Thunder, sustained air strikes on North Vietnam intended to stop the procession of supplies and soldiers to the
NLF in South Vietnam and to break the spirit of the Vietminh. The operation, which was scheduled to last eight
weeks but instead lasted three years, dropped over a million
tons of bombs on strategic locations, including roads, railway lines, and airfields. Johnson then sent the first U.S. combat troops to Southeast Asia; thirty-five hundred U.S.
Marines landed on the eastern shore of South Vietnam on
March 8, 1965.

In a televised address on April 7, 1965, President Johnson defended his escalation of the war, saying, "We will use
our power with restraint and with all the wisdom that we can
command. But we will use it." That same day he offered the
North Vietnamese a $1 billion Southeast Asia aid package to

participate in "unconditional discussions." North Vietnamese leaders rejected the offer and, three days after Johnson's speech, Ho Chi Minh retorted, "Johnson has loudly threatened to use violence to subdue our people. This is nothing but foolish illusion. Our people will never submit."

After their rejection of his aid package offer, Johnson realized that his bombing campaign was not intimidating the North Vietnamese Communists, and he agonized over whether to send more American soldiers to Vietnam. His advisers reminded him of American commitments to South Vietnam dating back to the Truman Doctrine and their belief that losing Vietnam would increase the threat of Communist domination in Asia. In July 1965, in attempting to win the war quickly, Johnson authorized sending 50,000 more American soldiers to Vietnam with 50,000 more to follow. By the end of 1965, he had escalated American military presence in Vietnam to include 184,000 American soldiers.

The Nature of Combat in Vietnam

U.S. military forces, led by General William C. Westmoreland, were poorly prepared for guerrilla warfare in Vietnam. Knowing that the American forces had superior firepower, the Communist forces used the same terrorist tactics that had defeated the French, fighting a defensive war without front lines or open battles. Makeshift booby traps caused an estimated 10 percent of American deaths in Vietnam, and terrorist activities were common near military bases and supposedly safe spaces for off-duty personnel. American troops resorted to search-and-destroy missions, sending small bands of soldiers into the jungles to flush out and kill guerrillas, "cleansing" regions only to have to return and cleanse the same region again.

The average American soldier in Vietnam was only nineteen years old, nearly eight years younger than the average soldier in World War II. Younger military recruits were usually poor, uneducated, unmotivated, and unprepared for the type of violence they faced in Southeast Asia. Many soldiers could not handle the frustration, brutality, and absurdity of the war. Racism became a serious problem for angry troops.

U.S. soldiers were not prepared for the guerrilla warfare in Vietnam and many didn't know how to handle emergency situations.

Drug use was common. Some men committed suicide, disobeyed orders, or, in an action termed *fragging*, killed unpopular officers with grenades.

In addition, frustrated soldiers found it difficult to identify the enemy since even Vietnamese women and children could kill soldiers with grenades and booby traps. On March 16, 1968, Lieutenant William Calley ordered his platoon to open fire on the village of My Lai. Among the nearly five hundred people whom Calley's men murdered were women, children, and elderly peasants. When the My Lai massacre was reported to the American public a year and a half later, a U.S. military court indicted and convicted Calley of murder, although President Gerald Ford eventually pardoned Calley in 1975.

From 1965 to 1968, General Westmoreland and other military and government leaders concealed morale problems with optimistic reports to Congress and the American people about the progress of the war and the demoralization of the enemy. Westmoreland later complained that Johnson had bullied him into giving news conferences and addresses to Congress to generate support for the war.

The Tet Offensive

On January 30, 1968, during Tet, the Vietnamese New Year, the Vietminh and Vietcong collectively began a massive military campaign against South Vietnamese strongholds. Communist forces attacked forty-four provincial capitals and sixty-four district capitals throughout South Vietnam. For a short time, the North Vietnamese Army controlled the city of Hue, and Vietcong forces occupied the U.S. embassy in Saigon. The three weeks of fighting in Hue may have been the bloodiest of the entire war. Communist forces lost thousands of soldiers, and before the arrival of American and South Vietnamese forces, the Vietminh and Vietcong killed an estimated three thousand civilians and civic leaders thought to be cooperating with the South Vietnamese.

At its conclusion, the Tet Offensive appeared to be a victory for the South Vietnamese and U.S. forces. In fighting that lasted nearly a month, the Communist forces lost some fifty thousand soldiers, one-fifth of their fighting population, and they never fully controlled any of the territories they attacked. However, the televised news of the fighting shocked American citizens and legislators and discredited the optimistic reports of American military leaders. Americans realized that the enemy was not demoralized and that victory in Southeast Asia would require more time, money, soldiers, and casualties. Antiwar sentiment grew stronger among the American people and in Congress.

On February 8, 1968, during the Tet Offensive, Senator Robert F. Kennedy, who had supported American intervention as a member of his brother John F. Kennedy's administration, declared, "The time has come to take a new look at the war in Vietnam." Kennedy was not alone in his uneasiness about the war in Southeast Asia. The U.S. Congress was divided between "doves," who opposed the war, and "hawks," who supported the war. Among the doves questioning American policy in Vietnam were Senators Ernest

Gruening, Wayne Morse, and George McGovern. J. William Fulbright, chairman of the Senate Foreign Relations Committee, had become particularly outspoken, arguing, "An unnecessary and immoral war deserves in its own right to be liquidated." Although doves were outnumbered in Congress by hawks, even hawks criticized Johnson's policies. Senator Barry Goldwater protested Johnson's policy of limited warfare, saying, "If the policy in Vietnam has left anything to be desired—and I am one who agrees that it has—it has been that it has not been firm enough."

A Division in the American House

In a televised speech on March 31, 1968, President Johnson announced that he would suspend the bombing of North Vietnam and that he would not run for reelection in the upcoming presidential election. Referring to the growing political turmoil in the United States, he conceded, "There is a division in the American house now."

This division began early in the war. Traditional pacifist groups started opposing American involvement after the Gulf of Tonkin incidents in 1964. Later, in the spring of 1965, students, professors, and concerned citizens gathered on campuses nationwide for "teach-ins," discussing the issues of the Vietnam War. The first teach-in occurred on March 24, 1965, on the University of Michigan campus at Ann Arbor. More than fifty university professors participated in the all-night event, reading, lecturing, and debating until late the next morning. One of the largest teach-ins was the Vietnam Day Teach-In at the University of California at Berkeley on May 21, 1965, where over thirty thousand participants over a thirty-six-hour period heard antiwar speakers, including Mario Savio of the Free Speech Movement, Black Panther Stokely Carmichael, child physician Benjamin Spock, Senator Ernest Gruening, and political writer I.F. Stone.

The first major organized antiwar protest was a march in Washington, D.C., on April 17, 1965. Although a radical student group, Students for a Democratic Society (SDS), had sponsored the event, twenty thousand people of all ages and backgrounds gathered to protest President Johnson's escalation of the war. Speakers included SDS president Paul Potter, who stated, "The people of Vietnam and the people in this demonstration are united in much more than a common concern that the war be ended. In both countries there are people struggling to build a movement that has the power to change their condition." Later, in November 1965, new SDS president Carl Oglesby blamed the war on the corruptions of American capitalism and "corporate liberalism" and reiterated Potter's call for an antiwar movement.

The antiwar movement that subsequently developed was characterized by diverse protest methods used by groups composed of activists of all ages with disparate backgrounds, motivations, and goals. Pacifists and religious leaders protested the immorality of the violence. Students, intellectuals, academicians, and civil servants criticized inconsistent, unethical, and unjust governmental practices and policies. Some radical activists advocated a revolutionary change in American cultural values while a few others, viewing themselves as freedom fighters, advocated a violent revolution in the United States.

Martin Luther King Jr. and other minority leaders protested the racial inequities and the costs of the war, arguing that American resources would be better spent at home. Early in 1967 King pleaded, "Somehow this madness must cease. . . . I speak for those whose land is being laid waste, whose homes are being destroyed, whose culture is being subverted. I speak for the poor of America who are paying the double price of smashed hopes at home, and dealt death and corruption in Vietnam. I speak as a citizen of the world, for the world as it stands aghast at the path we have taken."

Draft Resistance

In his speeches against the Vietnam War, King and other protesters often mentioned a pivotal issue of the war: the inequities of the draft policies of the Selective Service System. Under the law at that time, the Selective Service sent to local draft boards across America regional quotas for calling men into military service. The draft was mandatory for men between the ages of eighteen and thirty-five, although some deferrals were available. Some men claimed conscientious-objector (CO) status due to a general moral opposition to war until 1965, when the Supreme Court case *U.S. v. Seeger* eliminated that deferral. Undergraduate and graduate college students could defer induction until they finished school; however, in February 1966 the Selective Service determined that undergraduate college students who ranked lower in their class could be drafted. With 24 million men available for induction between 1961 and 1973, the change in draft policy was less a call for more soldiers than an attempt by government hawks to silence the growing college antiwar movement.

Protesters noted that many young men were being sent to die in a war when they were not even old enough to vote their opposition. Americans like King were also upset about the growing social inequality between those who could get draft deferments, usually men from wealthier backgrounds, and those who could not, usually poor minorities.

In March 1967 the draft-resistance movement, a powerful subset of the antiwar movement, began in California. In conjunction with another SDS-sponsored march on Washington in April 1967, organizers, including David Harris and folk singer Joan Baez, advocated a nationwide draft card burning, and on October 16, 1967, draft resisters organized a draft card turn-in day, returning their draft cards to the Selective Service. Thousands of men, refusing to fight for a cause they could not support, fled the country as "draft dodgers" or, refusing induction, were imprisoned for violating Selective Service laws before President Richard Nixon finally ended the draft in July 1973.

A Youth Movement Becomes a Mass Movement

During the early years of the war, most antiwar protesters were college students and most protests occurred on college campuses. For many young people, antiwar protest was part of the development of an American youth culture characterized by rebellion against conventional values, sexual experimentation, recreational drug use, and social activism.

As time passed and the war continued, more ordinary citizens participated in antiwar protests. The moratorium movement advocated a one-day suspension of work and school every month until troops were withdrawn from Vietnam; millions of Americans nationwide stayed home or attended antiwar demonstrations during the first moratorium in October 1969.

Soldiers were also protesting the war. The Vietnam Veterans Against the War (VVAW) formed in 1967 and soon had chapters throughout the United States and in Vietnam. In early 1971 the VVAW held its Winter Soldier Investigations to testify to the public about the activities of American soldiers in Vietnam. In April 1971, as more than two hundred thousand Vietnam veterans gathered in Washington, D.C., to protest the war, John Kerry, representing the VVAW before the Senate Foreign Relations Committee, delivered a graphic description of American activities in Vietnam, including confessions by American soldiers of atrocities they had committed.

In the summer of 1971 the *New York Times* began publishing the Pentagon Papers, documents stolen by former Defense Department official Daniel Ellsberg. The Pentagon Papers were a secret history of U.S. policy in Vietnam, revealing how the U.S. government had consistently deceived the American public about the progress of the war. The revelations of the Pentagon Papers and of the VVAW deepened public distrust of the federal government, and by 1972 polls indicated that more than 70 percent of Americans were demanding that President Richard Nixon end the war.

Nixon and Vietnamization

Before Richard Nixon won the presidency in November 1968, he had campaigned against Hubert Humphrey with the promise that he had a secret plan to achieve an "honorable peace" in Southeast Asia and to withdraw American troops from Vietnam. Upon becoming president in 1969, Nixon began withdrawing American troops from Vietnam while negotiating with North Vietnam at the Paris peace talks. In a televised address in November 1969, he revealed his secret plan to the nation. Advocating the "Vietnamization" of the war, Nixon planned to continue withdrawing troops while shifting responsibility for the war effort to the South Vietnamese army.

Nevertheless, Nixon's "peace" policies actually escalated the war. In March 1969, a few weeks after his inauguration, Nixon ordered Operation Menu, a series of secret air strikes against Vietminh and Vietcong targets in Cambodia. Then, on April 29, 1970, American troops invaded Cambodia to attack Communist sanctuaries. Reports about the clandestine attacks on Cambodia outraged antiwar protesters, who organized strikes and protests at college campuses nationwide. On May 4, 1970, as thousands of students gathered on the main lawn at Kent State University to protest Nixon's Cambodian invasion, the Ohio National Guard clashed with protesters and, firing into the crowd, killed four students. Many shocked activists concluded that the Kent State fiasco demonstrated the willingness of American people to kill their own children to stop political protest.

In June 1970 Congress repealed the Gulf of Tonkin Resolution and Nixon withdrew American troops from Cambodia. Then, in December, Congress passed the Cooper-Church Bill, forbidding the use of U.S. troops in Laos or Cambodia. Nixon, however, continued to order bombing missions in both countries in support of South Vietnamese operations while steadily withdrawing American troops. When he had taken office in 1969, 540,000 Americans were serving in Vietnam. By December 1970, American soldiers in Vietnam numbered 280,000, and by December 1971, the number had decreased to 150,000.

Moving Toward Peace

Peace discussions had begun during Lyndon B. Johnson's presidency. Johnson declined to run for reelection in 1968 so that he might devote his full efforts, unimpeded by politics, to the quest for peace in Vietnam. Johnson's representatives, Cyrus Vance and Averell Harriman, began meeting in Paris with representatives from North Vietnam, and in October 1968 negotiators reached an agreement to end both the U.S. bombing of North Vietnam and all North Vietnamese attacks on South Vietnamese cities. Accordingly, President Johnson halted the bombing of North Vietnam, finally ending Operation Rolling Thunder on October 31, 1968.

Richard Nixon, campaigning against Hubert Humphrey for the presidency, heard about the agreement and contacted Johnson, accusing him of trying to throw the election to Humphrey. Johnson responded, through Secretary of State Dean Rusk, by briefing Nixon about the Paris peace negotiations. Fearing that the Johnson administration might end the war before he won the election, Nixon secretly contacted South Vietnamese leaders and advised them to hold out for a better deal from the Nixon administration, effectively sabotaging the Paris peace talks. On November 2, 1968, South Vietnamese president Nguyen Van Thieu announced that his representatives would no longer attend the Paris negotiations, and on November 6, 1968, Richard Nixon won the U.S. presidential election. As a result, the fighting in Vietnam continued for more than four years.

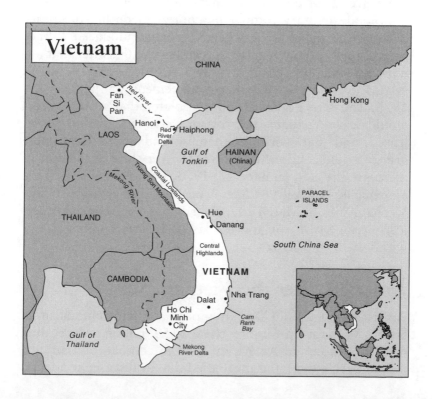

During 1969 President Nixon progressively escalated the air war against North Vietnam while withdrawing American troops and requesting peace talks with the North Vietnamese. In August 1969 he wrote to Ho Chi Minh asking for secret negotiations between the United States and North Vietnam. Ho agreed, but several days later, on September 3, Ho Chi Minh died at the age of seventy-nine. In 1970 Nixon sent National Security adviser Henry Kissinger to secret discussions in Paris with North Vietnamese negotiator Lu Duc Tho. Peace talks failed when neither side would compromise. During the next three years military activity escalated as North Vietnamese and U.S. forces attempted to force concessions from each other. The largest and most effective Communist military strike was the Easter Offensive assault on South Vietnamese cities. President Nixon's retaliation, a massive bombing campaign, drew harsh criticism from American citizens. Nixon defended his tactics in a televised address on April 26, 1972, calling Americans to unite in seeking, "not the peace of surrender, but peace with honor."

Bloody military campaigns continued during the peace talks until October 1972, when Kissinger announced, "Peace is at hand." Although peace agreements stalled after that announcement, the third attempt succeeded, and President Nixon announced a cease-fire agreement on January 23, 1973. The Paris Peace Accords stipulated that all U.S. forces would leave Vietnam, that prisoners of war would be released, and that North Vietnamese and South Vietnamese armies would continue to control territory held at the time of the cease-fire. On January 27, 1973, both parties signed the agreement, officially ending American participation in the Vietnam War. In March 1973 North Vietnam released American prisoners of war and the last American combat troops withdrew from Vietnam.

America After the Vietnam War

America's failed Cold War attempt to contain communism in South Vietnam cost more than $150 billion. More than forty-five thousand Americans died in combat, and an estimated twelve thousand more died due to disease, accidental

death, and other causes. In addition, over twenty-five hundred soldiers were missing in action (MIA) and many Americans thought that North Vietnam still held U.S. soldiers as
prisoners of war (POWs); the POW/MIA issue would aggra-
vate U.S. policy makers for the rest of the century.

On the home front, Americans remained divided over the
issues of the Vietnam War for decades. The postwar years
were characterized by public distrust of government, bitterness, shame, and emotional suffering. In a healing gesture,
President Jimmy Carter, on the day after his inauguration,
pardoned most Vietnam War draft evaders.

Nearly 3 million veterans returned to America irrepara-
bly damaged by their service in Vietnam. Many veterans
struggled for years with divorces, spousal and child abuse,
psychological disorders, physical ailments, drug addictions,
and unemployment. By some estimates, more than half of all
homeless Americans were Vietnam War veterans. In addition, returning veterans found that the American people were
painfully divided about the Vietnam War and were unwilling
or unable to welcome them home.

In another healing gesture on November 11, 1982, nearly
ten years after their return, the United States publicly honored Vietnam veterans with the dedication of a memorial in
Washington, D.C. Stretching 492 feet, the Vietnam Veterans
Memorial consists of a black granite wall containing the
names of every soldier who died in Vietnam.

Vietnam After the American War

The war between North Vietnam and South Vietnam continued after American troops withdrew as both sides violated
the Paris Peace Accords. In the spring of 1975 North Vietnam, aware that the United States would not send aid to
South Vietnam because of political unrest at home, invaded
and quickly took control of South Vietnam. On April 23,
1975, President Gerald Ford, unable to persuade Congress to
assist the South Vietnamese, declared the war "finished,"
and on April 30, 1975, all remaining Americans were evacu-
ated from the U.S. embassy in Saigon. Ho Chi Minh's goal of
a fully unified Vietnam was finally realized.

Then, in 1977, the Pol Pot regime in Cambodia invaded parts of Vietnam in an attempt to recapture land that had belonged to Cambodia centuries earlier. Vietnam retaliated in 1978 by invading Cambodia and establishing a new Cambodian government. China, Cambodia's ally, demanded that Vietnam withdraw, and when Vietnam refused, China invaded northern Vietnam in 1979. After sixteen days, China withdrew, but the war with China cost Vietnam sixty thousand men, alienated its former ally, and further damaged an ailing economy.

An Economic War

After withdrawing military forces, the United States began another war against Vietnam—a war that was, in some ways, more ruthless than the military war had been. For almost two decades the United States led an international economic embargo against Vietnam, almost destroying an already crippled economy. In 1977 the Carter administration negotiated with the Vietnamese to normalize relations in exchange for a fuller accounting for POW/MIAs and the release of former South Vietnamese officials from prison. When negotiations failed, the United States extended the embargo, treating Vietnam as an enemy, vetoing Hanoi's attempts to join the United Nations, and barring economic and diplomatic relations with Vietnam for Americans and American allies. Subsequent attempts to lift the embargo were hindered by a powerful American POW/MIA lobby and by lingering bitterness about the war.

The Vietnamese Communists, who had militarily defeated the Japanese, the French, the Americans, the South Vietnamese, the Cambodians, and the Chinese, were less successful at economic warfare. When the government nationalized all industries and organized farmers into cooperatives in 1978, it accelerated economic disaster as production dropped and food shortages resulted. Threatened with starvation, many Vietnamese people rebelled against the government and more than a million "boat people" fled the country in any available boat to become refugees in other countries. In 1981, the United States organized a program with other nations to protect the refugees, providing $2 million in support. Many of the refugees had been business owners and their departure deprived Vietnam of critical business expertise, intensifying its financial problems during the early 1980s.

In 1986 Vietnam's Sixth Party Congress introduced political and economic reforms designed to stimulate production, reduce inflation, and improve relations with the United States; Vietnam withdrew from Cambodia and introduced more reforms in 1989. Many American allies lifted the embargo and began trading with Vietnam. Pressured by business leaders and Vietnamese American citizens, President George Bush considered normalizing relations but refused to do so until the Vietnamese provided a fuller accounting for missing American soldiers. The Vietnamese government protested that more than three hundred thousand of its own soldiers were still missing, but it agreed to greater cooperation with the Bush administration.

Finally, in 1994, President Bill Clinton, who had protested against the war as a student, lifted the trade embargo, normalizing relations with Vietnam and ending the economic war. Members of Congress who supported Clinton's decision included Senators John McCain, John Kerry, and Bob Kerrey—all Vietnam veterans. In 1995 Clinton's secretary of state, Warren Christopher, opened the U.S. embassy in Hanoi, and in 1997 Clinton appointed Douglas "Pete" Peterson, who had been a prisoner of war in Hanoi during the war, to be the first postwar ambassador to Vietnam. Ambassador Peterson immediately announced two priorities: "The fullest possible accounting of persons missing from the war" and "to help Vietnam become a prosperous country."

Vietnam's economy, stimulated by American investment, dramatically improved as Vietnam continued to move toward a market economy by reforming its trade policies, opening its economy to foreign exchange, and reducing state control of the economy. With the lifting of the embargo, tourism became one of Vietnam's brightest economic prospects as thousands of American students, businesspeople, Vietnam War veterans, and tourists visited Vietnam every year.

President Clinton became the first U.S. president to visit Hanoi when he addressed students at Vietnam National University on November 17, 2000. Referring to Vietnam's Declaration of Independence in which Ho Chi Minh quoted the U.S. Declaration of Independence, Clinton reviewed the two-hundred-year history of relations between the United States and Vietnam. Then, speaking about the benefits of globalization and economic interdependence, he said, "Both of our nations were born with a Declaration of Independence. This trade agreement is a form of declaration of interdependence, a clear, unequivocal statement that prosperity in the 21st century depends upon a nation's economic engagement in the rest of the world. . . . May our children learn from us that good people, through respectful dialogue, can discover and rediscover their common humanity, and that a painful, painful past can be redeemed in a peaceful and prosperous future."

CHAPTER ONE

Prewar
Diplomacy

The Vietnamese Declaration of Independence

Ho Chi Minh

In 1941, Vietnamese native Ho Chi Minh returned to his homeland after nearly thirty years of living in foreign lands. At the time of his return, the Vietnamese people had suffered under French colonial rule since the 1850s and under Japanese occupation since September 1940. Intent on liberating Vietnam from both the French and the Japanese, "Uncle Ho" organized the League for Vietnamese Independence, also known as the Vietminh, and allied his forces with American forces in fighting against the Japanese for the remainder of World War II. In August 1945, at the end of the war, Ho led the "August Revolution," a general uprising against the regime of Vietnamese Emperor Bao Dai, then proclaimed the independence of Vietnam.

Although known to most Americans as a Communist revolutionary, Ho Chi Minh expressed an appreciation of American independence and self-determination and a dedication to Vietnamese independence more than to any particular ideology. On September 2, 1945, speaking in Hanoi before an estimated half million of his countrymen and accompanied by some of his American military allies, Ho Chi Minh proclaims Vietnamese independence and announces the formation of the Provisional Government of the Democratic Republic of Vietnam. By quoting both the Declaration of Independence of the United States and the Declaration of the French Revolution on the Rights of

Excerpted from *Declaration of Independence of the Democratic Republic of Vietnam*, by Ho Chi Minh, September 2, 1945.

Man and the Citizen, Ho suggests that, despite his Communist Party affiliation, he represents a local revolt against French colonial rule, anticipating the debate that would continue for the rest of the century about whether Ho's revolutionaries were freedom fighters or Communist aggressors.

A ll men are created equal. They are endowed by their Creator with certain inalienable rights, among these are Life, Liberty, and the pursuit of Happiness.

This immortal statement was made in the Declaration of Independence of the United States of America in 1776. In a broader sense, this means: All the peoples on the earth are equal from birth, all the peoples have a right to live, to be happy and free.

The Declaration of the French Revolution made in 1791 on the Rights of Man and the Citizen also states: "All men are born free and with equal rights, and must always remain free and have equal rights." Those are undeniable truths.

The French Imperialists

Nevertheless, for more than eighty years, the French imperialists, abusing the standard of Liberty, Equality, and Fraternity, have violated our Fatherland and oppressed our fellow-citizens. They have acted contrary to the ideals of humanity and justice. In the field of politics, they have deprived our people of every democratic liberty.

They have enforced inhuman laws; they have set up three distinct political regimes in the North, the Center and the South of Vietnam in order to wreck our national unity and prevent our people from being united.

They have built more prisons than schools. They have mercilessly slain our patriots; they have drowned our uprisings in rivers of blood. They have fettered public opinion; they have practiced obscurantism against our people. To weaken our race they have forced us to use opium and alcohol.

In the fields of economics, they have fleeced us to the

backbone, impoverished our people, and devastated our land.

They have robbed us of our rice fields, our mines, our forests, and our raw materials. They have monopolized the issuing of bank-notes and the export trade.

They have invented numerous unjustifiable taxes and reduced our people, especially our peasantry, to a state of extreme poverty.

They have hampered the prospering of our national bourgeoisie; they have mercilessly exploited our workers.

In the autumn of 1940, when the Japanese Fascists violated Indochina's [Laos, Cambodia, and Vietnam] territory to establish new bases in their fight against the Allies, the French imperialists went down on their bended knees and handed over our country to them.

Thus, from that date, our people were subjected to the double yoke of the French and the Japanese. Their sufferings and miseries increased. The result was that from the end of last year to the beginning of this year, from Quang Tri province to the North of Vietnam, more than two million of our fellow-citizens died from starvation. On March 9, the French troops were disarmed by the Japanese. The French colonialists either fled or surrendered, showing that not only were they incapable of "protecting" us, but that, in the span of five years, they had twice sold our country to the Japanese.

On several occasions before March 9, the Vietminh League urged the French to ally themselves with it against the Japanese. Instead of agreeing to this proposal, the French colonialists so intensified their terrorist activities against the Vietminh members that before fleeing they massacred a great number of our political prisoners detained at Yen Bay and Cao Bang.

Not withstanding all this, our fellow-citizens have always manifested toward the French a tolerant and humane attitude. Even after the Japanese putsch of March 1945, the Vietminh League helped many Frenchmen to cross the frontier, rescued some of them from Japanese jails, and protected French lives and property.

From the autumn of 1940, our country had in fact ceased to be a French colony and had become a Japanese possession.

After the Japanese had surrendered to the Allies, our

whole people rose to regain our national sovereignty and to found the Democratic Republic of Vietnam.

The truth is that we have wrested our independence from the Japanese and not from the French.

The French have fled, the Japanese have capitulated, Emperor Bao Dai has abdicated. Our people have broken the chains which for nearly a century have fettered them and have won independence for the Fatherland. Our people at the same time have overthrown the monarchic regime that has reigned supreme for dozens of centuries. In its place has been established the present Democratic Republic.

For these reasons, we, members of the Provisional Government, representing the whole Vietnamese people, declare that from now on we break off all relations of a colonial character with France; we repeal all the international obligations that France has so far subscribed to on behalf of Vietnam and we abolish all the special rights the French have unlawfully acquired in our Fatherland.

The whole Vietnamese people, animated by a common purpose, are determined to fight to the bitter end against any attempt by the French colonialists to reconquer their country.

We are convinced that the Allied nations which at Tehran and San Francisco have acknowledged the principles of self-determination and equality of nations, will not refuse to acknowledge the independence of Vietnam.

A people who have courageously opposed French domination for more than eighty years, a people who have fought side by side with the Allies against the Fascists during these last years, such a people must be free and independent.

For these reasons, we, members of the Provisional Government of the Democratic Republic of Vietnam, solemnly declare to the world that Vietnam has the right to be a free and independent country—and in fact it is so already. The entire Vietnamese people are determined to mobilize all their physical and mental strength, to sacrifice their lives and property in order to safeguard their independence and liberty.

The Truman Doctrine

Harry S. Truman

After the second World War, a new kind of international political tension quickly developed. As revolutions in Eastern Europe and in Asia brought countries under Communist rule, the democratic countries, seeing communism as a threat to democracy, formulated policies to resist the spread of Communist influence worldwide. However, after a war that ended with the use of atomic weapons, any international conflict held devastating potential; therefore, postwar foreign policy requirements included the necessity of limiting warfare to forestall nuclear disaster. The resulting tension in international relations became known as the Cold War.

Vice President Harry S. Truman had become president of the United States during World War II upon the death of President Franklin D. Roosevelt a month before Germany's surrender in 1945. After the end of World War II, Truman became concerned about the worldwide spread of Communist influence. Due to his apprehension about Ho Chi Minh's Communist Party ties, Truman refused to recognize Vietnamese independence and supported French colonial claims in Vietnam instead. Later, in response to Communist threats in Greece and Turkey, Truman formulated an American policy regarding Communist aggression. In a speech before Congress on March 12, 1947, Truman states that it will be American policy to consider acts of aggression against free peoples anywhere in the world as threatening to United States security and that the United States will support free peoples to resist subjugation by internal minorities or by external aggressors. Although Truman specifies that U.S. support

---

Excerpted from Harry S. Truman's address to the United States Congress, March 12, 1947.

will be primarily economic and financial aid, his policy statement, known as the Truman Doctrine, soon became a justification for American participation in the Korean War and would eventually become a justification for American military intervention in Vietnam.

O ne of the primary objectives of the foreign policy of the United States is the creation of conditions in which we and other nations will be able to work out a way of life free from coercion. This was a fundamental issue in the war with Germany and Japan. Our victory was won over countries which sought to impose their will, and their way of life, upon other nations.

To ensure the peaceful development of nations, free from coercion, the United States has taken a leading part in establishing the United Nations. The United Nations is designed to make possible lasting freedom and independence for all its members. We shall not realize our objectives, however, unless we are willing to help free peoples to maintain their free institutions and their national integrity against aggressive movements that seek to impose upon them totalitarian regimes. This is no more than a frank recognition that totalitarian regimes imposed upon free peoples, by direct or indirect aggression, undermine the foundations of international peace and hence the security of the United States.

The peoples of a number of countries of the world have recently had totalitarian regimes forced upon them against their will. The Government of the United States has made frequent protests against coercion and intimidation, in violation of the Yalta agreement, in Poland, Rumania, and Bulgaria. I must also state that in a number of other countries there have been similar developments.

Choosing Paths

At the present moment in world history nearly every nation must choose between alternative ways of life. The choice is too often not a free one.

One way of life is based upon the will of the majority, and is distinguished by free institutions, representative government, free elections, guarantees of individual liberty, freedom of speech and religion, and freedom from political oppression.

The second way of life is based upon the will of a minority forcibly imposed upon the majority. It relies upon terror and oppression, a controlled press and radio, fixed elections, and the suppression of personal freedoms.

I believe that it must be the policy of the United States to support free peoples who are resisting attempted subjugation by armed minorities or by outside pressures.

I believe that we must assist free peoples to work out their own destinies in their own way.

I believe that our help should be primarily through economic and financial aid which is essential to economic stability and orderly political processes.

The world is not static, and the status quo is not sacred. But we cannot allow changes in the status quo in violation of the Charter of the United Nations by such methods as coercion, or by such subterfuges as political infiltration. In helping free and independent nations to maintain their freedom, the United States will be giving effect to the principles of the Charter of the United Nations. . . .

The seeds of totalitarian regimes are nurtured by misery and want. They spread and grow in the evil soil of poverty and strife. They reach their full growth when the hope of a people for a better life has died.

We must keep that hope alive.

The free peoples of the world look to us for support in maintaining their freedoms.

If we falter in our leadership, we may endanger the peace of the world—and we shall surely endanger the welfare of this Nation.

Great responsibilities have been placed upon us by the swift movement of events.

I am confident that the Congress will face these responsibilities squarely.

The United States Should Consider Intervention in Vietnam

John Foster Dulles

When John Foster Dulles became the United States secretary of state for President Dwight D. Eisenhower in 1953, French forces had been at war with Ho Chi Minh's Vietminh guerrillas in Vietnam since 1946. In 1950, the Truman administration had officially recognized the French-supported Bao Dai regime in South Vietnam and had authorized U.S. military aid to the French forces against the Vietminh. As the chief architect of the Eisenhower administration's Cold War strategy to implement the Truman Doctrine, Dulles authored the "containment" policy of using U.S. economic, diplomatic, and military resources to counter Communist aggression anywhere it emerged in the world. In September 1953, President Eisenhower escalated U.S. involvement by approving $785 million in military aid to the Bao Dai regime, and the United States was paying nearly 80 percent of French expenses in Vietnam by 1954. In March 1954, Vietminh guerrilla fighters attacked the U.S.-backed French forces at Dien Bien Phu in North Vietnam near the Laos border, creating anxiety that a French defeat would result in a Communist takeover of Vietnam. The Eisenhower administration began considering U.S. military intervention in support of the French.

Excerpted from John Foster Dulles's speech before the Overseas Press Club, March 29, 1954.

In an address to the Overseas Press Club in New York
City on March 29, 1954, during the siege of Dien Bien
Phu, John Foster Dulles explains that the United States
supports the development of independence in Southeast
Asia, but that the war in Vietnam is part of a worldwide
pattern of Communist-supported aggression against free
nations. Since Southeast Asia is strategically important to
American security, Dulles recommends a strong United
States response to the Communist threat in Vietnam.
Dulles's suggestion of potential U.S. military intervention
in Vietnam, delivered less than a year after the end of the
Korean War, galvanized opposition in a United States Con-
gress concerned about American participation in another
war; two future presidents, Senator John F. Kennedy and
Senator Lyndon B. Johnson, spoke in opposition to Dulles.

I ndochina is important for many reasons. First-and always first are the human values. About 30 million people
are seeking for themselves the dignity of self-government.
Until a few years ago, they formed merely a French depen-
dency. Now, their three political units—Vietnam, Laos and
Cambodia—are exercising a considerable measure of independent political authority within the French Union. Each of
the three is now recognized by the United States and by more
than 30 other nations. They signed the Japanese Peace Treaty
with us. Their independence is not yet complete. But the
French Government last July declared its intention to complete that independence, and negotiations to consummate
that pledge are actively under way.

The United States is watching this development with
close attention and great sympathy. We do not forget that we
were a colony that won its freedom. We have sponsored in
the Philippines a conspicuously successful development of
political independence. We feel a sense of kinship with those
everywhere who yearn for freedom.

The Communists are attempting to prevent the orderly
development of independence and to confuse the issue before
the world. The Communists have, in these matters, a regular

line which [Soviet leader Josef] Stalin laid down in 1924.

The scheme is to whip up the spirit of nationalism so that it becomes violent. That is done by professional agitators. Then the violence is enlarged by Communist military and technical leadership and the provision of military supplies. In these ways, international Communism gets a strangle-hold on the people and it uses that power to "amalgamate" the peoples into the Soviet orbit.

"Amalgamation" is [Soviet leader] Lenin's and Stalin's word to describe their process.

"Amalgamation" is now being attempted in Indochina under the ostensible leadership of Ho Chi Minh. He was indoctrinated in Moscow. He became an associate of the Russian, [legendary Russian agent Mikhail] Borodin, when the latter was organizing the Chinese Communist Party which was to bring China into the Soviet orbit. Then Ho transferred his activities to Indochina.

The United States backed the South Vietnamese as part of the "containment" policy of using U.S. economic, diplomatic, and military resources to fight communism.

Those fighting under the banner of Ho Chi Minh have largely been trained and equipped in Communist China. They are supplied with artillery and ammunition through the

Soviet-Chinese Communist bloc. Captured material shows that much of it was fabricated by the Skoda Munition Works in Czechoslovakia and transported across Russia and Siberia and then sent through China into Vietnam. Military supplies for the Communist armies have been pouring into Vietnam at a steadily increasing rate.

Military and technical guidance is supplied by an estimated 2,000 Communist Chinese. They function with the forces of Ho Chi Minh in key positions—in staff sections of the High Command, at the division level and in specialized units such as signal, engineer, artillery and transportation.

In the present stage, the Communists in Indochina use nationalistic anti-French slogans to win local support. But if they achieved military or political success, it is certain that they would subject the People to a cruel Communist dictatorship taking its orders from Peiping and Moscow.

The Scope of the Danger

The tragedy would not stop there. If the Communist forces won uncontested control over Indochina or any substantial part thereof, they would surely resume the same pattern of aggression against other free peoples in the area.

The propagandists of Red China and Russia make it apparent that the purpose is to dominate all of Southeast Asia.

Southeast Asia is the so-called "rice bowl" which helps to feed the densely populated region that extends from India to Japan. It is rich in many raw materials, such as tin, oil, rubber and iron ore. It offers industrial Japan potentially important markets and sources of raw materials.

The area has great strategic value. Southeast Asia is astride the most direct and best developed sea and air routes between the Pacific and South Asia. It has major naval and air bases. Communist control of Southeast Asia would carry a grave threat to the Philippines, Australia and New Zealand, with whom we have treaties of mutual assistance. The entire Western Pacific area, including the so-called "offshore island chain", would be strategically endangered.

President Eisenhower appraised the situation last Wednesday when he said that the area is of "transcendent importance."

The U.S. Position

The United States has shown in many ways its sympathy for the gallant struggle being waged in Indochina by French forces and those of the Associated States [of French Indochina]. Congress has enabled us to provide material aid to the established governments and their peoples. Also, our diplomacy has sought to deter Communist China from open aggression in that area.

President [Dwight D.] Eisenhower, in his address of April 16, 1953, explained that a Korean armistice would be a fraud if it merely released aggressive armies for attack elsewhere. I said last September that if Red China sent its own army into Indochina, that would result in grave consequences which might not be confined to Indochina.

Recent statements have been designed to impress upon potential aggressors that aggression might lead to action at places and by means of free world choosing, so that aggression would cost more than it could gain.

The Chinese Communists have, in fact, avoided the direct use of their own Red armies in open aggression against Indochina. They have, however, largely stepped up their support of the aggression in that area. Indeed, they promote that aggression by all means short of open invasion.

Under all the circumstances it seems desirable to clarify further the United States position.

Under the conditions of today, the imposition on Southeast Asia of the political system of Communist Russia and its Chinese Communist ally, by whatever means, would be a grave threat to the whole free community. The United States feels that that possibility should not be passively accepted, but should be met by united action. This might involve serious risks. But these risks are far less than those that will face us a few years from now, if we dare not be resolute today.

The free nations want peace. However, peace is not had merely by wanting it. Peace has to be worked for and planned for. Sometimes it is necessary to take risks to win peace just as it is necessary in war to take risks to win victory. The chances for peace are usually bettered by letting a potential aggressor know in advance where his aggression could lead him.

The United States Should Be Cautious About Intervention in Vietnam

John F. Kennedy

John F. Kennedy, a Harvard graduate and a decorated veteran of World War II, began public service in 1946 as a United States congressman and became a senator in 1952. As a congressman, Kennedy had opposed American intervention in the Korean War and, as a senator, he opposed American intervention in Vietnam. On March 29, 1954, when John Foster Dulles called for a strong American response to the Communist threat in Vietnam, France was on the verge of defeat at Dien Bien Phu after fighting Ho Chi Minh's forces for eight years with massive U.S. assistance.

On April 6, 1954, when he rose in Congress to respond to Dulles's speech, Kennedy had been in Congress since the beginning of the French war in Vietnam and, as a congressman, he had toured Southeast Asia in 1951 for several weeks. In this speech, Kennedy argues against American intervention in Vietnam, claiming that no amount of U.S. military assistance can be successful in Vietnam because the Communist rebels have the sympathy and covert support of the Vietnamese people. He suggests that American policy should be to support Vietnamese independence and, at the same time, encourage anti-Communist sentiment. Although his speech predicted the major problems of the Vietnam War ten years before

Excerpted from John F. Kennedy's address before the United States Senate, April 6, 1954.

American combat troops landed in Vietnam, by the time
of his inaugural address in 1961, Kennedy had become a
supporter of the war and, as president, he expanded U.S.
commitments in Vietnam.

Mr. President [of the Senate], the time has come for
the American people to be told the blunt truth
about Indochina.

I am reluctant to make any statement which may be mis-
interpreted as unappreciative of the gallant French struggle at
Dien Bien Phu and elsewhere; or as partisan criticism of our
Secretary of State just prior to his participation in the delicate
deliberations in Geneva. Nor, as one who is not a member of
those committees of the Congress which have been briefed—
if not consulted—on this matter, do I wish to appear impetu-
ous or an alarmist in my evaluation of the situation. But the
speeches of President [Dwight] Eisenhower, Secretary [John
Foster] Dulles, and others have left too much unsaid, in my
opinion—and what has been left unsaid is the heart of the
problem that should concern every citizen. For if the American people are, for the fourth time in this century, to travel
the long and tortuous road of war—particularly a war which
we now realize would threaten the survival of civilization—
then I believe we have a right—a right which we should have
hitherto exercised—to inquire in detail into the nature of the
struggle in which we may become engaged, and the alternative to such struggle. Without such clarification the general
support and success of our policy is endangered.

The Geneva Negotiations

In as much as Secretary Dulles has rejected, with finality, any
suggestion of bargaining on Indochina in exchange for recognition of Red China, those discussions in Geneva which concern that war may center around two basic alternatives:

The first is a negotiated peace, based either upon partition of the area between the forces of the Viet Minh and the
French Union, possibly along the 16th parallel; or based

upon a coalition government in which Ho Chi Minh is represented. Despite any wishful thinking to the contrary, it should be apparent that the popularity and prevalence of Ho Chi Minh and his following throughout Indochina would cause either partition or a coalition government to result in eventual domination by the Communists.

The second alternative is for the United States to persuade the French to continue their valiant and costly struggle; an alternative which, considering the current state of opinion in France, will be adopted only if the United States pledges increasing support. Secretary Dulles' statement that the "imposition in southeast Asia of the political system of Communist Russia and its Chinese Communist ally . . . should be met by united action" indicates that it is our policy to give such support; that we will, as observed by the *New York Times*, "fight if necessary to keep southeast Asia out of their hands"; and that we hope to win the support of the free countries of Asia for united action against communism in Indochina, in spite of the fact that such nations have pursued since the war's inception a policy of cold neutrality. . . .

Certainly, I, for one, favor a policy of a "united action" by many nations whenever necessary to achieve a military and political victory for the free world in that area, realizing full well that it may eventually require some commitment of our manpower. . . .

But to pour money, material, and men into the jungles of Indochina without at least a remote prospect of victory would be dangerously futile and self-destructive. Of course, all discussion of "united action" assumes the inevitability of such victory; but such assumptions are not unlike similar predictions of confidence which have lulled the American people for many years and which, if continued, would present an improper basis for determining the extent of American participation. . . .

In February 1954, Defense Secretary Charles Erwin Wilson said that a French victory was "both possible and probable" and that the war was going "fully as well as we expected it to at this stage. I see no reason to think Indochina would be another Korea." Also in February, Under Secretary of State [Walter Bedell] Smith stated that:

The military situation in Indochina is favorable. . . . Contrary to some reports, the recent advances made by the Viet Minh are largely "real estate" operations. . . . Tactically, the French position is solid and the officers in the field seem confident of their ability to deal with the situation.

In later March, Admiral Arthur Radford, Chairman of the Joint Chiefs of Staff, stated that "the French are going to win." And finally, in a press conference some days prior to his speech to the Overseas Press Club in New York, Secretary of State Dulles stated that he did not "expect that there is going to be a Communist victory in Indochina"; that "in terms of Communist domination of Indochina, I do not accept that as a probability.". . .

Despite this series of optimistic reports about eventual victory, every member of the Senate knows that such victory today appears to be desperately remote, to say the least, despite tremendous amounts of economic and materiel aid from the United States, and despite a deplorable loss of French Union manpower. The call for either negotiations or additional participation by other nations underscores the remoteness of such a final victory today, regardless of the outcome at Dien Bien Phu. It is, of course, for these reasons that many French are reluctant to continue the struggle without greater assistance; for to record the sapping effect which time and the enemy have had on their will and strength in that area is not to disparage their valor. If "united action" can achieve the necessary victory over the forces of communism, and thus preserve the security and freedom of all Southeast Asia, then such united action is clearly called for. But if, on the other hand, the increase in our aid and the utilization of our troops would only result in further statements of confidence without ultimate victory over aggression, then now is the time when we must evaluate the conditions under which that pledge is made.

I am frankly of the belief that no amount of American military assistance in Indochina can conquer an enemy which is everywhere and at the same time nowhere, "an enemy of the people" which has the sympathy and covert support of the people. . . .

Moreover, without political independence for the Associated States [of French Indochina], the other Asiatic nations have made it clear that they regard this as a war of colonialism; and the "united action" which is said to be so desperately needed for victory in that area is likely to end up as unilateral action by our own country. Such intervention, without participation by the armed forces of the other nations of Asia, without the support of the great masses of the people of the Associated States, with increasing reluctance and discouragement on the part of the French—and, I might add, with hordes of Chinese Communist troops poised just across the border in anticipation of our unilateral entry into their kind of battleground—such intervention, Mr. President, would be virtually impossible in the type of military situation which prevails in Indochina.

This is not a new point, of course. In November of 1951, I reported upon my return from the Far East as follows:

> In Indochina we have allied ourselves to the desperate effort of a French regime to hang on to the remnants of empire. There is no broad, general support of the native Vietnam government among the people of that area. To check the southern drive of communism makes sense but not only through reliance on the force of arms. The task is rather to build strong native non-Communist sentiment within these areas and rely on that as a spearhead of defense rather than upon the legions of General de Lattre. To do this apart from and in defiance of innately nationalistic aims spells foredoomed failure.

In June of last year, I sought an amendment to the Mutual Security Act which would have provided for the distribution of American aid, to the extent feasible, in such a way as to encourage the freedom and independence desired by the people of the Associated States. My amendment was soundly defeated on the grounds that we should not pressure France into taking action on this delicate situation; and that the new French government could be expected to make "a decision which would obviate the necessity of this kind of amendment or resolution." The distinguished majority leader [William Knowland] assured us that "We will all work, in conjunction with our great ally, France, toward the freedom of the people of those states."

Every year we are given three sets of assurances: First, that the independence of the Associated States is now complete; second, that the independence of the Associated States will soon be completed under steps "now" being undertaken; and, third, that military victory for the French Union forces in Indochina is assured, or is just around the corner, or lies two years off. But the stringent limitations upon the status of the Associated States as sovereign states remain; and the fact that military victory has not yet been achieved is largely the result of these limitations. Repeated failure of these prophecies has, however, in no way diminished the frequency of their reiteration, and they have caused this nation to delay definitive action until now the opportunity for any desirable solution may well be past.

It is time, therefore, for us to face the stark reality of the difficult situation before us without the false hopes which predictions of military victory and assurances of complete independence have given us in the past. The hard truth of the matter is, first, that without the wholehearted support of the peoples of the Associated States, without a reliable and crusading native army with a dependable officer corps, a military victory, even with American support, in that area is difficult if not impossible, of achievement; and, second, that the support of the people of that area cannot be obtained without a change in the contractual relationships which presently exist between the Associated States and the French Union.

If the French persist in their refusal to grant the legitimate independence and freedom desired by the peoples of the Associated States; and if those peoples and the other peoples of Asia remain aloof from the conflict, as they have in the past, then it is my hope that Secretary Dulles, before pledging our assistance at Geneva, will recognize the futility of channeling American men and machines into that hopeless internecine struggle.

The facts and alternatives before us are unpleasant, Mr. President. But in a nation such as ours, it is only through the fullest and frankest appreciation of such facts and alternatives that any foreign policy can be effectively maintained. In an era of supersonic attack and atomic retaliation, extended public debate and education are of no avail, once such a policy must be implemented. The time to study, to doubt, to review, and revise is now, for upon our decisions now may well rest the peace and security of the world, and, indeed, the very continued existence of mankind. And if we cannot entrust this decision to the people, then, as Thomas Jefferson once said: "If we think them not enlightened enough to exercise their control with a wholesome discretion, the remedy is not to take it from them but to inform their discretion by education."

GREAT
SPEECHES
IN
HISTORY

American
Intervention

U.S. Foreign Policy Is Leading Toward War in Vietnam

Wayne Morse

On August 2, 1964, North Vietnamese patrol boats attacked an American destroyer, the *Maddox*, in the Gulf of Tonkin off the eastern coast of North Vietnam. President Lyndon B. Johnson and his advisers had decided to respond with a letter of protest to Hanoi when the *Maddox* reported a second attack on August 4. Johnson ordered retaliatory air strikes on patrol boat bases in North Vietnam and requested that Congress authorize American combat operations in Southeast Asia.

On August 7, 1964, Congress passed the Gulf of Tonkin Resolution, a joint congressional resolution giving the president unprecedented authority to conduct military operations in Vietnam. The House of Representatives passed the resolution unanimously and the Senate passed it by a vote of eighty-eight to two, with Senators Ernest Gruening of Alaska and Wayne Morse of Oregon voting against it. During the congressional debate over the resolution, four-term United States Senator Wayne Morse, who had served in Congress since 1945, challenged Secretary of Defense Robert McNamara's account of the Tonkin Gulf events, reminding him that the North Vietnamese patrol boat attacks had been provoked by U.S. presence in Tonkin Bay.

After Congress granted Johnson war-making powers, Senator Morse began a series of opposition speeches that

Excerpted from Wayne Morse's speech at Syracuse University, December 14, 1964.

would continue for the remainder of his Senate term. In
this address at Syracuse University in December 1964,
Morse details the history of an American policy in South
Vietnam that seems to be leading the United States into
war. He relates that President Franklin D. Roosevelt, believing that French dominion should not be restored, intended to support independence for Vietnam before his
death. Instead, Morse says, the United States adopted a
policy, which he characterizes as a form of American
colonialism, of protecting U.S. interests at the expense of
those of the Vietnamese people. He replays the Tonkin
Gulf events as evidence of a hypocritical discrepancy between announced and real U.S. interests, and he urges
President Lyndon B. Johnson to lead the United States
away from the threatening morass of war in Vietnam.

   Senator Morse's antiwar speeches were among the
earliest protests against the Vietnam War, encouraging
and validating the antiwar movement and requiring public explanations from government policy makers. His eloquent, informed, and insistent criticisms alerted the
American people, the press, and his colleagues in Congress to the increasing dangers of war in Vietnam and to
government deceptions about the conduct of the war.
Many U.S. congressmen later credited Senator Morse
with the emergence of antiwar sentiment in Congress.

I n fact, no new evidence has been offered to change the assessment that the great bulk of the Vietcong rebels were
   local residents, that close to 90 percent of their weapons
were captured from Government sources, and that their civil
war against the Government would continue whether or not
it received aid or leadership from North Vietnam.

   But the 100 percent expansion of the South Vietnamese
Air Force and the drum-beating in both Washington and
Saigon about alleged infiltration from North Vietnam, suggest to these experienced ears that air attacks by U.S. jets
flown by United States and Vietnamese pilots will soon com-
mence in Laos, as they may already have begun in the demil-

itarized zone of North Vietnam. What this will accomplish, no one has explained. . . .

Origins of Present Policy

One of the most astonishing elements in the discussions of this policy is the number of Washington officials who will tell you that getting into South Vietnam was a hideous mistake, but once involved we have no choice but to continue. One wonders how much blood they are willing to spill to pursue a policy they recognize was fallacious from the beginning.

But I would like to go back to the end of World War II and examine the history of American relations with southeast Asia to see just how our policy led us to the present perilous situation.

Twenty years ago almost to the very month, the subject of postwar American policy in southeast Asia came in for study in the high levels of Government. A State Department memorandum to President [Franklin D.] Roosevelt suggested that positive announcements should be made of American policy toward the former colonial areas of southeast Asia being liberated from Japanese occupation. It suggested that specific dates for their self-government be set as objectives of American policy.

We know from [Secretary of State] Cordell Hull's memoirs that President Roosevelt heartily endorsed that policy. He believed that French dominion over Indochina should not be restored. At the Cairo and Teheran Conferences he urged that it be placed under an international trusteeship as a final step toward independence. . . .

Today we are paying the price for our failure to carry out that policy. Within 10 years of the end of the war, the British, the Dutch, and the French largely recognized, after years of war and the expenditure of billions of dollars, that colonialism is a thing of the past. It is the United States that has failed to recognize what Mr. Roosevelt knew to be true: The era of white rule in Asia is finished, whether it takes the form of economic exploitation through direct rule or the form of manipulating governments to protect what we regard to be our interest—the postwar American form of colonialism.

Roosevelt's policy died with him. Our primary interest became one of bowing to French wishes in all international matters to guarantee her support and participation in NATO, and we began financing the French effort to recapture Indochina. We put over $1¼ billion into that futile struggle. And when the French finally gave up, we took it over ourselves. . . .

The Geneva Accord

When France finally gave up the struggle in Indochina, the United States refused to sign the Geneva Accord of 1954, which ended the war. And we prevailed upon a new government we had chosen to back in South Vietnam not to sign it either. We began to send military aid early in 1955, and we, along with South and North Vietnam, were found by the International Control Commission to be in violation of the treaty.

The sad truth is that the threats of leading American officials to make war on China and the present war crisis, are the logical end of the dismal road in Indochina that John Foster Dulles set us upon in 1954. After failing in his efforts to keep the French fighting on in Indochina, despite American aid to their war effort and the promise of direct U.S. military action, Dulles refused to put the signature of the United States on the Geneva agreement of 1954 which marked the end of French rule there. South Vietnam also declined to sign. The most the United States said about the 1954 agreement was that we would recognize it as international law and regard violations with grave concern and as seriously threatening international peace and security. . . .

For 10 years we have claimed that North Vietnam was violating the accord by sending in help to the rebels against the South Vietnamese Government. But our solution was not to go to the parties who signed the agreement and who were responsible for its enforcement. Nor did we go to the United Nations, the sole international body with jurisdiction over threats to the peace.

Instead we multiplied our own violations by joining in the fighting. Each time we increase the number of American boys sent to that country to "advise" the local troops we violate the Geneva agreement of 1954. Every jet plane, every helicopter, every naval vessel we furnish South Vietnam or man with American servicemen is a violation, and so is every military base and airstrip we have constructed there.

Yet we hypocritically proclaim to ourselves and the world that we are there only to enforce the Geneva agreement. . . .

Immediately upon the signing of the 1954 agreement, the United States began to support the new government of South Vietnam in a big way. In the letter President [Dwight D.] Eisenhower wrote President [Ngo Dinh] Diem, a letter still serving as the basis for our policy in 1964, aid was pledged to Diem, and in turn, "the Government of the United States expects that this aid will be met by performance on the part of the Government of Vietnam in undertaking needed reforms."

No Freedom or Democracy in South Vietnam

In 1964, President [Lyndon] Johnson refers to that letter as the basis for our aid, but the part about reforms has long since been forgotten.

In the decade following 1954, the United States for all practical purposes made a protectorate out of South Vietnam. Its new government immediately became financially dependent upon us; as rebellion against it grew, our level of aid was stepped up. By 1961, we had to send 15,000 American troops as "advisers" to the local military forces. Today, the figure is 22,000. . . .

Now we are faced with the collapse of the government we have been supporting. It is becoming obvious that it was not a case of our aiding an established government; but of having created and maintained in office a whole series of governments that have had little or no support among the people.

We have been making covert war in southeast Asia for some time, instead of seeking to keep the peace. It was inevitable and inexorable that we would have to engage in overt acts of war as we are now doing. . . .

The United States is, of course, a full partner in the Government of South Vietnam. I am satisfied that since 1954 we have been a provocateur of military conflict in southeast Asia and marched away from our obligations to international law.

In recent months, evidence has mounted that both the Pentagon and the State Department were preparing to escalate the war into Laos and North Vietnam. American forces in nearby bases in the Philippines and Okinawa have been poised for air attacks on Laos and North Vietnam. The 7th Fleet has moved into the South China Sea and the Gulf of Tonkin, while the entry of ground forces through Thailand into Laos has been prepared.

Last August, vessels we had furnished to South Vietnam were used to shell two islands in the Tonkin Gulf belonging to North Vietnam. Meanwhile, American naval vessels patrolled a few miles seaward in international waters.

Those vessels were pursued by northern PT [patrol] boats. Anticipating an attack, our destroyers began the exchange of fire while they were still some 3 miles away. After the second such incident, a well-planned retaliatory air raid was carried out against the ports harboring the PT boats.

This raid was not self-defense on our part; it was supposed to be a "lesson" to North Vietnam. It was supposed to give her a taste of what would happen to her if she did not cease and desist from what we regard as her interference in the affairs of South Vietnam. Today, one can only conclude that the lesson was lost. . . .

The fact that it is really American interests and not the interests of South Vietnam about which we are concerned is coming to the surface. Now, we hear that American prestige cannot take the blow of a retreat from South Vietnam; and if the war cannot be won there, then we must display our strength somewhere else. Our objective is no longer to help another people, but to maintain an American military presence on the mainland of Asia.

The discrepancy between our announced interests and our real interests is the source of much of our difficulty with American public opinion about southeast Asia. As long as the fiction could be maintained that we were helping a people remain "free," support for almost any U.S. involvement could be expected. But the disintegration of the political fabric of South Vietnam has exposed this discrepancy.

The signs from official Washington indicate a recognition among even the most ardent advocates of this U.S. policy in Vietnam that it has been a failure. Of the alternatives now being discussed, the one espoused so long by General [Maxwell] Taylor and Secretary [Robert] McNamara for increased U.S. aid is rarely heard.

That is because the preponderance of American money and military equipment is already so heavy that additional increments could not affect the situation. South Vietnam—at least the third or so of it still under Government control—has for many months been completely saturated with U.S. money, U.S. military equipment, and U.S. advisers, both political and military.

Still the tide runs against us. Still the political condition of the country deteriorates, and still the Vietcong raid with greater success and audacity. . . .

How Much Further?

How much further do we want to dig ourselves into this pit, started by the Eisenhower administration and deepened by the Kennedy administration?

That question is going to have to be answered by President Johnson alone. It is too bad that all these chickens have all come home to roost on his doorstep; but there they are.

The resolution passed last August by Congress gave the President a blank check to use force in Asia. As a legal statement it means little; but it was sought and given as a political backstop. On two other occasions, similar resolutions authorizing a President to use armed force in given areas led right straight to war. One was with Mexico in 1846 and a second was with Spain in 1898. Those resolutions, like the current one, were supposed to prevent war by warning an adversary of our intentions. But both had to be followed by declarations of war. . . .

The further we go in expanding the war—the more agreements we violate and the more people we kill in the name of peace—the more military opposition we harden against us in North Vietnam and China—the more we alienate ourselves from the now-Communist nations in that part of the world—

the more impossible any peaceful solution becomes.

In the last 10 years we have learned that we are not masters of events in Vietnam, despite our billions of dollars and our thousands of troops on the scene. It has not been shown that any stepped-up investment of blood or money will make us masters.

It still is not too late for President Johnson to lead the American people out of this morass. Whether he leads us out or further in, will be the first great test of his administration.

The United States Must Fight Communist Aggression in Vietnam

Lyndon B. Johnson

Two days after assuming the presidency following President John F. Kennedy's assassination on November 22, 1963, Lyndon B. Johnson reaffirmed American support for the new South Vietnamese government that had assumed power after the overthrow of the Diem regime by a military coup earlier that month. At the time, over sixteen thousand American soldiers served as military advisers to the South Vietnamese army. By mid-1964, Johnson had increased the number of military advisers in Vietnam to over twenty-seven thousand. Following the Gulf of Tonkin resolution, which gave him almost unlimited authority to conduct war in Southeast Asia, Johnson began to escalate American military intervention. In early 1965, he authorized Operation Rolling Thunder, the sustained bombing of North Vietnam. Then, in March 1965, the first American combat troops, thirty-five hundred U.S. Marines, landed near Da Nang, South Vietnam. Antiwar protest in the United States, which had begun after the Gulf of Tonkin incidents, quickly escalated, especially on university campuses.

In response to antiwar sentiment expressed by Senators Ernest Gruening and Wayne Morse, by students, and by pacifist groups, President Johnson explained his rea-

---

Excerpted from Lyndon B. Johnson's speech at Johns Hopkins University, April 7, 1965.

sons for sending American troops to Vietnam in a speech at Johns Hopkins University on April 7, 1965. Characterizing the North Vietnamese attack on South Vietnam as part of a worldwide pattern of Communist aggression, Johnson declares that the American objective is the independence of South Vietnam, invites North Vietnam to join the United States in cooperative economic development of Southeast Asia, and shares his dream of a world free from war. On the day of the speech, Johnson offered one billion dollars in economic development aid to Vietnam if North Vietnam would participate in "unconditional discussions." North Vietnamese Prime Minister Pham Van Dong rejected the offer the next day and North Vietnamese Communist leader Ho Chi Minh denounced Johnson's offer in an angry speech three days later.

Johnson's speech outlined the strategy that he would follow in the Vietnam War for the remainder of his term in office. It was a variation on John Foster Dulles's Cold War strategy of bringing the enemy to the brink of destruction using massive American military power before offering to negotiate. Johnson and his advisers would discover over the next three years how badly they had underestimated their enemy.

Tonight Americans and Asians are dying for a world where each people may choose its own path to change. This is the principle for which our ancestors fought in the valleys of Pennsylvania. It is the principle for which our sons fight tonight in the jungles of Vietnam.

Vietnam is far away from this quiet campus. We have no territory there, nor do we seek any. The war is dirty and brutal and difficult. And some 400 young men, born into an America that is bursting with opportunity and promise, have ended their lives on Vietnam's steaming soil.

Why must we take this painful road?

Why must this Nation hazard its ease, and its interest, and its power for the sake of a people so far away?

We fight because we must fight if we are to live in a world

where every country can shape its own destiny. And only in such a world will our own freedom be finally secure.

This kind of world will never be built by bombs or bullets. Yet the infirmities of man are such that force must often precede reason, and the waste of war, the works of peace.

We wish that this were not so. But we must deal with the world as it is, if it is ever to be as we wish.

The Nature of the Conflict

The world as it is in Asia is not a serene or peaceful place.

The first reality is that North Vietnam has attacked the independent nation of South Vietnam. Its object is total conquest.

Of course, some of the people of South Vietnam are participating in attack on their own government. But trained men and supplies, orders and arms, flow in a constant stream from north to south.

This support is the heartbeat of the war.

And it is a war of unparalleled brutality. Simple farmers are the targets of assassination and kidnapping. Women and children are strangled in the night because their men are loyal to their government. And helpless villages are ravaged by sneak attacks. Large-scale raids are conducted on towns, and terror strikes in the heart of cities.

The confused nature of this conflict cannot mask the fact that it is the new face of an old enemy.

Over this war—and all Asia—is another reality: the deepening shadow of Communist China. The rulers in Hanoi are urged on by Peking. This is a regime which has destroyed freedom in Tibet, which has attacked India, and has been condemned by the United Nations for aggression in Korea. It is a nation which is helping the forces of violence in almost every continent. The contest in Vietnam is part of a wider pattern of aggressive purposes.

Why Are We in Vietnam?

Why are these realities our concern? Why are we in South Vietnam?

We are there because we have a promise to keep. Since 1954 every American President has offered support to the people of South Vietnam. We have helped to build, and we have helped to defend. Thus, over many years, we have made a national pledge to help South Vietnam defend its independence.

And I intend to keep that promise.

To dishonor that pledge, to abandon this small and brave nation to its enemies, and to the terror that must follow, would be an unforgivable wrong.

We are also there to strengthen world order. Around the globe, from Berlin to Thailand, are people whose well-being rests, in part, on the belief that they can count on us if they are attacked. To leave Vietnam to its fate would shake the confidence of all these people in the value of an American commitment and in the value of America's word. The result would be increased unrest and instability, and even wider war.

We are also there because there are great stakes in the balance. Let no one think for a moment that retreat from Vietnam would bring an end to conflict. The battle would be renewed in one country and then another. The central lesson of our time is that the appetite of aggression is never satisfied. To withdraw from one battlefield means only to prepare for the next. We must say in southeast Asia—as we did in Europe—in the words of the Bible: "Hitherto shalt thou come, but no further."

There are those who say that all our effort there will be futile—that China's power is such that it is bound to dominate all southeast Asia. But there is no end to that argument until all of the nations of Asia are swallowed up.

There are those who wonder why we have a responsibility there. Well, we have it there for the same reason that we have a responsibility for the defense of Europe.

World War II was fought in both Europe and Asia, and when it ended we found ourselves with continued responsibility for the defense of freedom.

Our Objective in Vietnam

Our objective is the independence of South Vietnam and its freedom from attack. We want nothing for ourselves—only that the people of South Vietnam be allowed to guide their own country in their own way.

We will do everything necessary to reach that objective. And we will do only what is absolutely necessary.

In recent months attacks on South Vietnam were stepped up. Thus, it became necessary for us to increase our response and to make attacks by air. This is not a change of purpose. It is a change in what we believe that purpose requires.

We do this in order to slow down aggression.

We do this to increase the confidence of the brave people of South Vietnam who have bravely borne this brutal battle for so many years with so many casualties.

And we do this to convince the leaders of North Vietnam—and all who seek to share their conquest—of a very simple fact:

We will not be defeated.

We will not grow tired.

We will not withdraw, either openly or under the cloak of a meaningless agreement.

We know that air attacks alone will not accomplish all of these purposes. But it is our best and prayerful judgment that they are a necessary part of the surest road to peace.

We hope that peace will come swiftly. But that is in the hands of others besides ourselves. And we must be prepared for a long continued conflict. It will require patience as well as bravery, the will to endure as well as the will to resist.

I wish it were possible to convince others with words of what we now find it necessary to say with guns and planes: Armed hostility is futile. Our resources are equal to any challenge. Because we fight for values and we fight for principles, rather than territory or colonies, our patience and our determination are unending.

Once this is clear, then it should also be clear that the only path for reasonable men is the path of peaceful settlement.

Such peace demands an independent South Vietnam—securely guaranteed and able to shape its own relationships to all others—free from outside interference—tied to no alliance—a military base for no other country.

These are the essentials of any final settlement.

We will never be second in the search for such a peaceful settlement in Vietnam.

There may be many ways to this kind of peace: in discussion or negotiation with the governments concerned; in large groups or in small ones; in the reaffirmation of old agreements or their strengthening with new ones.

We have stated this position over and over again fifty times and more, to friend and foe alike. And we remain ready, with this purpose, for unconditional discussions.

And until that bright and necessary day of peace we will try to keep conflict from spreading. We have no desire to see thousands die in battle—Asians or Americans. We have no desire to devastate that which the people of North Vietnam have built with toil and sacrifice. We will use our power with restraint and with all the wisdom that we can command.

But we will use it.

This war, like most wars, is filled with terrible irony. For what do the people of North Vietnam want? They want what their neighbors also desire: food for their hunger; health for their bodies; a chance to learn; progress for their country; and an end to the bondage of material misery. And they would find all these things far more readily in peaceful association with others than in the endless course of battle.

A Cooperative Effort for Development

These countries of southeast Asia are homes for millions of impoverished people. Each day these people rise at dawn and struggle through until the night to wrestle existence from the soil. They are often wracked by disease, plagued by hunger, and death comes at the early age of 40.

Stability and peace do not come easily in such a land. Neither independence nor human dignity will ever be won, though, by arms alone. It also requires the work of peace. The American people have helped generously in times past in these works. Now there must be a much more massive effort to improve the life of man in that conflict-torn corner of our world.

The first step is for the countries of southeast Asia to associate themselves in a greatly expanded cooperative effort for development. We would hope that North Vietnam would take its place in the common effort just as soon as peaceful cooperation is possible.

The United Nations is already actively engaged in development in this area. As far back as 1961 I conferred with our authorities in Vietnam in connection with their work there. And I would hope tonight that the Secretary General of the United Nations [U Thant] could use the prestige of his great office, and his deep knowledge of Asia, to initiate, as soon as possible, with the countries of that area, a plan for cooperation in increased development.

For our part I will ask the Congress to join in a billion dollar American investment in this effort as soon as it is underway.

And I would hope that all other industrialized countries, including the Soviet Union, will join in this effort to replace despair with hope, and terror with progress. The task is nothing less than to enrich the hopes and the existence of more than a hundred million people. And there is much to be done.

The vast Mekong River can provide food and water and power on a scale to dwarf even our own TVA [Tennessee Valley Authority]. The wonders of modern medicine can be spread through villages where thousands die every year from lack of care.

Schools can be established to train people in the skills that are needed to manage the process of development.

And these objectives, and more, are within the reach of a cooperative and determined effort.

I also intend to expand and speed up a program to make available our farm surpluses to assist in feeding and clothing the needy in Asia. We should not allow people to go hungry and wear rags while our own warehouses overflow with an abundance of wheat and corn, rice and cotton.

So I will very shortly name a special team of outstanding, patriotic, distinguished Americans to inaugurate our participation in these programs. This team will be headed by Mr. Eugene Black, the very able former President of the World Bank.

In areas that are still ripped by conflict, of course development will not be easy.

Peace will be necessary for final success. But we cannot and must not wait for peace to begin this job.

The Dream of World Order

This will be a disorderly planet for a long time. In Asia, as elsewhere, the forces of the modern world are shaking old ways and uprooting ancient civilizations.

There will be turbulence and struggle and even violence. Great social change—as we see in our own country now—does not always come without conflict.

We must also expect that nations will on occasion be in dispute with us. It may be because we are rich, or powerful; or because we have made some mistakes; or because they honestly fear our intentions. However, no nation need ever fear that we desire their land, or to impose our will, or to dictate their institutions.

But we will always oppose the effort of one nation to conquer another nation.

We will do this because our own security is at stake.

But there is more to it than that. For our generation has a dream. It is a very old dream. But we have the power and now we have the opportunity to make that dream come true.

For centuries nations have struggled among each other. But we dream of a world where disputes are settled by law and reason. And we will try to make it so.

For most of history men have hated and killed one another in battle. But we dream of an end to war. And we will try to make it so.

For all existence most men have lived in poverty, threatened by hunger. But we dream of a world where all are fed and charged with hope. And we will help to make it so.

The ordinary men and women of North Vietnam and South Vietnam—of China and India—of Russia and America—are brave people. They are filled with the same proportions of hate and fear, of love and hope. Most of them want the same things for themselves and their families. Most of them do not want their sons to ever die in battle, or to see their homes, or the homes of others, destroyed. Well, this can be their world yet. Man now has the knowledge—always before denied—to make this planet serve the real needs of the people who live on it.

I know this will not be easy. I know how difficult it is for reason to guide passion, and love to master hate. The complexities of this world do not bow easily to pure and consistent answers.

But the simple truths are there just the same. We must all try to follow them as best we can. . . .

Have We Done Enough?

Every night before I turn out the lights to sleep I ask myself this question: Have I done everything that I can do to unite this country? Have I done everything I can to help unite the world, to try to bring peace and hope to all the peoples of the world? Have I done enough?

Ask yourselves that question in your homes and in this hall tonight. Have we, each of us, all done all we could? Have we done enough?

We may well be living in the time foretold many years ago when it was said: "I call heaven and earth to record this day against you, that I have set before you life and death, blessing and cursing: therefore choose life, that both thou and thy seed may live."

This generation of the world must choose: destroy or build, kill or aid, hate or understand.

We can do all these things on a scale never dreamed of before.

Well, we will choose life. In so doing we will prevail over the enemies within man, and over the natural enemies of all mankind.

The United States Is the Aggressor in Vietnam

Ho Chi Minh

Immediately after the end of World War II, Ho Chi Minh wrote several letters to U.S. President Harry S. Truman reminding him of the support the Vietnamese people had given the American military in Southeast Asia during the war and requesting that the United States recognize the Democratic Republic of Vietnam and oppose French colonial claims in Vietnam. Truman and his advisers, however, suspicious of Ho Chi Minh's Communist Party affiliation and fearing that Vietnam would fall under Communist influence, ignored Ho's appeals and, instead, began supplying military aid to the French. In January 1950, Communist China began sending military advisers and modern weapons to Ho's Vietminh guerrillas.

By the time the U.S. combat troops landed in South Vietnam on March 8, 1965, the Vietminh forces had become a modern conventional army, renamed the Army of the Democratic Republic of Vietnam under General Vo Nguyen Giap. Giap's guerrilla soldiers had not only helped the allies drive out the Japanese during World War II, but had also defeated the French at Dien Bien Phu and had beaten the much larger and better equipped U.S.-financed South Vietnamese army in virtually every encounter.

In a speech before the Vietnamese National Assembly on April 10, 1965, an apparent response to President Lyndon Johnson's address at Johns Hopkins University

---

Excerpted from Ho Chi Minh's speech before the Vietnamese National Assembly, April 10, 1965.

three days earlier, Ho Chi Minh condemns the United
States as an aggressor violating the Geneva Agreements in
South Vietnam. He asserts that the only way for the
United States to attain peace in Vietnam is to respect the
Geneva Agreements by withdrawing from Vietnam. Ho
characterizes Johnson as hypocritical to offer one billion
dollars in development money after devastating his country and massacring his people. About Johnson's threats to
use violence, he says, "This is nothing but foolish illusion. Our people will never submit." With this speech,
Ho Chi Minh demonstrated how little he was intimidated
by American military power, how confident he was about
his own military forces, how aware he was of the political situation in the United States, how dedicated he remained to the cause of Vietnamese independence, and
how much his position had hardened with regard to negotiating with the United States.

O
ur National Assembly is holding the present session in
a very urgent situation but in enthusiasm and full confidence. Our struggle against American aggression for
national salvation is surging up everywhere. Many great successes have been recorded in both North and South Vietnam.

Over the past ten years, the U.S. imperialists and their
henchmen have carried out an extremely ruthless war, causing so much mourning to our compatriots in South Vietnam.
During the last few months, they have been frenziedly expanding the war to the North of our country. In defiance of
the 1954 Geneva Agreements and international law, they
have sent hundreds of aircraft and dozens of warships to
bomb and strafe North Vietnam unremittingly. Laying bare
themselves their piratical face, the U.S. aggressors are
brazenly encroaching upon our territory. They attempt to use
the might of weapons to enslave our thirty million compatriots. But they have been grossly mistaken. They will certainly
meet with ignominious defeat.

Ours are a heroic people. For more than ten years now,
our fourteen million countrymen in the South have been en-

during every hardship and sacrifice and struggling very valiantly. Starting with bare hands, they have seized weapons from the enemy to fight against him, scored victory after victory and are now constantly on the offensive, inflicting on the U.S. aggressors and the traitors ever-greater setbacks and driving them into ever-deeper bog. The heavier their defeats, the more cruel means they use, such as napalm and toxic gases to massacre people. It is because they are bogged down in the South that they furiously attack the North.

As the "thief crying stop thief" is a customary trick of theirs, the U.S. imperialists who are the aggressors have impudently slandered North Vietnam as committing "aggression" on South Vietnam. Saboteurs of peace and of the Geneva Agreements, they have brazenly declared that because they wished to "restore peace" and "defend the

Many South Vietnamese families lost their homes and many children were orphaned as a result of the Vietcong attacks.

Geneva Agreements" they sent U.S. troops to our country to kill and destroy. They, who have been devastating our country, and massacring our people, hypocritically stated that they would grant one billion dollars to the people in Vietnam and other South-East Asian countries to develop their economy and improve their livelihood.

The Threat of American Violence

U.S. President [Lyndon B.] Johnson has also loudly threatened to use violence to subdue our people. This is nothing but foolish illusion. Our people will never submit. . . .

We love peace but we are not afraid of war. We are resolved to drive away the U.S. aggressors to defend the freedom, independence and territorial integrity of our fatherland.

Our people throughout the country are firmly confident that with their militant solidarity, valiant spirit and creative resourcefulness and with the sympathy and support of the world peoples they will surely lead this great resistance war to complete victory.

Our people are very grateful to, and highly value the fraternal solidarity and devoted assistance of, the socialist countries—especially, the Soviet Union and China—the people on all continents who are actively backing our struggle against the U.S. imperialist aggressors—the most cruel enemy of mankind.

With regard to the Lao and Cambodian peoples who are courageously struggling against the U.S. imperialists and their valets, our people constantly strengthen solidarity with them and wholeheartedly support them.

We warmly welcome the youth of various countries, who have volunteered to go to Vietnam and join us in fighting the U.S. aggressors.

The American people have been duped by the propaganda of their government which has extorted from them billions of dollars for war purposes. Thousands of American youths—their sons and brothers—have met a tragic death or been pitifully wounded on the Vietnamese battlefields thousands of miles from the United States. At present, many mass organizations and personalities in the United States are demanding that their government stop at once the unjust war and withdraw immediately U.S. troops from South Vietnam. Our people are determined to drive away the U.S. imperialists—always express our friendship with the progressive American people.

The Government of the Democratic Republic of Vietnam once again solemnly declares its unswerving stand, that is, to resolutely defend Vietnam's independence, sovereignty, unity and territorial integrity. Vietnam is one country, the Vietnamese people are one nation; nobody is allowed to infringe upon this sacred right. The U.S. imperialists must respect the Geneva Agreements, withdraw from South Vietnam, and immediately stop the attacks on North Vietnam. That is the only measure to settle the war in Vietnam, to implement the 1954 Geneva Agreements, to defend peace in Indochina and South-East Asia. There is no other solution. And that is the answer of our people and government to the U.S. imperialists.

The World Peoples' Front

Our people are living in a most glorious period of history. Our country has the great honor of being an outpost of the socialist camp and of the world peoples' front against imperialism, colonialism and neo-colonialism.

Our people are fighting and making sacrifices not only for their own freedom and independence, but also for the freedom and independence of other peoples, for world peace.

On the battlefront against the U.S. imperialist aggressors, our people's task is very heavy but very glorious as well.

At present, to oppose U.S. aggression for national salvation is the most sacred task of every Vietnamese patriot. Under the leadership of the National Front for Liberation—the sole authentic representative of the South Vietnamese people—the heroic population and fighters in South Vietnam are marching forward to achieve ever-greater successes so as to liberate the South and defend the North. . . .

Let all of us single-mindedly unite millions like one man, and be determined to defeat the U.S. aggressors.

For the future of our Fatherland, for the happiness of our people, let all compatriots and fighters throughout the country valiantly march forward.

The Vietnamese People Will Defeat the Imperialist Aggressors

Le Duan

When Ho Chi Minh returned to Vietnam in 1941, he selected a small group of trustworthy and talented individuals to lead the Vietminh. Among Ho's chosen few was Le Duan, a young railroad employee turned revolutionary. In 1959, he became general secretary of the Vietnamese Workers Party and Ho Chi Minh's chief deputy. After the formation of the National Liberation Front in South Vietnam in December 1960, he became a primary spokesperson for that organization and, upon Ho Chi Minh's death in 1969, Le Duan became the leader of the North Vietnamese people.

In the following speech given in the summer of 1965, weeks before a major U.S. mobilization in Vietnam, Le Duan prepares the Vietnamese people for the fighting to come. He explains that the mobilization of three hundred thousand to four hundred thousand American troops will expose the colonialist mission of the United States. He argues, in an apparent reference to the American antiwar movement, that "influential sectors" in the United States will oppose such a mission. In addition, he reasons, the United States cannot fight a protracted war because the imperialist foreign policy of the United States has distributed American resources throughout the world. Le Duan's speech, delivered four months after the initial mo-

Excerpted from Le Duan's speech before a Special Conference of the Vietnamese People, July 6, 1965.

bilization of U.S. combat troops in South Vietnam, was
not only prophetic about American participation in the
war, but also demonstrated a strategic sophistication that
U.S. military and foreign policy analysts continued to un-
derestimate in an enemy that they would persist in characterizing as "a handful of guerrillas."

I f the U.S. puts 300–400,000 troops into the South, it will
have stripped away the face of its neocolonial policy and
revealed the face of an old style colonial invader, contrary
to the whole new-style annexation policy of the U.S. in the
world at present. Thus, the U.S. will not be able to maintain its
power with regard to influential sectors of the United States.

If the U.S. itself directly enters the war in the South it will
have to fight for a prolonged period with the people's army of
the South, with the full assistance of the North and of the Socialist bloc. To fight for a prolonged period is a weakness of
U.S. imperialism. The Southern revolution can fight a protracted war, while the U.S. can't, because American military,
economic and political resources must be distributed throughout the world. If it is bogged down in one place and can't
withdraw, the whole effort will be violently shaken. The U.S.
would lose its preeminence in influential sectors at home and
create openings for other competing imperialists, and lose the
American market.

Therefore at present, although the U.S. can immediately
send 300,000 to 400,000 troops at once, why must the U.S.
do it step by step? Because even if it does send many troops
like that, the U.S. would still be hesitant; because that would
be a passive policy full of contradictions; because of fear of
protracted war, and the even stronger opposition of the
American people and the world's people, and even of their allies who would also not support widening the war.

The War of Destruction on North Vietnam

With regard to the North, the U.S. still carries out its war of
destruction, primarily by its air force: Besides bombing mili-

tary targets, bridges and roads to obstruct transport and communications, the U.S. could also indiscriminately bomb economic targets, markets, villages, schools, hospitals, dikes, etc., in order to create confusion and agitation among the people.

But the North is determined to fight back at the U.S. invaders in a suitable manner, determined to punish the criminals, day or night, and determined to make them pay the blood debts which they have incurred to our people in both zones. The North will not flinch for a moment before the destructive acts of the U.S., which could grow increasingly made with every passing day. The North will not count the cost but will use all of its strength to produce and fight, and endeavor to help the South.

For a long time, the Americans have boasted of the strength of their air force and navy but during five to six months of directly engaging in combat with the U.S. in the North, we see clearly that the U.S. cannot develop that strength in relation to the South as well as in relation to the North, but revealed more clearly every day its weak points. We have shot down more than 400 of their airplanes, primarily with rifles, anti-aircraft guns, the high level of their hatred of the aggressors, and the spirit of determination to defeat the U.S. invaders.

Therefore, if the U.S. sends 300,000–400,000 troops into the South, and turns special war into direct war in the South, escalating the war of destruction in the North, they still can't hope to avert defeat, and the people of both North and South will still be determined to fight and determined to win.

CHAPTER
THREE

GREAT
SPEECHES
IN
HISTORY

The War Abroad

The Vietnam War Is an External Aggression, Not a Local Conflict

George W. Ball

In March 1965, President Lyndon B. Johnson sent thirty-five hundred American combat troops into Vietnam, and by the end of the year U.S. military personnel in Vietnam numbered almost 184,000. Antiwar protest also escalated during 1965, beginning with the first teach-ins, gatherings to discuss issues of the war, and including a march on Washington, D.C., and nationwide antiwar demonstrations. Antiwar sentiment grew in Congress, as well, and on January 28, 1966, Senator J. William Fulbright began hearings of the Senate Foreign Relations Committee to investigate the legitimacy of the Vietnam War.

A central argument of antiwar protest speeches was that what the U.S. government characterized as Communist aggression was really a nationalist revolution by the South Vietnamese people, led by the National Liberation Front, seeking self-determination. On January 30, 1966, Undersecretary of State George W. Ball responded to these protests on behalf of the Johnson administration in the following address before the Northwestern University Alumni Association. He supports President Johnson's contention that the war in Vietnam is not a local revolt by indigenous rebels seeking freedom, but part of a worldwide pattern of Communist aggression.

From 1961 to 1966, George Ball served as the under-

Excerpted from George W. Ball's speech before the Northwestern University Alumni Association, January 30, 1966.

secretary of state for the administrations of both President John F. Kennedy and President Lyndon B. Johnson. Due to his pessimism concerning American participation in the Vietnam War, he became known as the devil's advocate for both those administrations and was characterized as the loyal opposition. In a memo to President Johnson in July 1965, Ball forcefully advised against sending American troops into Vietnam. In a secret meeting later that month, he flatly stated, "We cannot win, Mr. President. This war will be long and protracted." To Johnson's concern about losing credibility by withdrawing, Ball responded, "The worst blow would be that the mightiest power on earth is unable to defeat a handful of guerrillas." In public, nonetheless, George Ball explained and defended the government's policies.

T he beginning of wisdom with regard to Vietnam is to recognize that what Americans are fighting in the jungles and rice paddies of that unhappy land is not a local conflict—an isolated war that has meaning only for one part of the world.

We can properly understand the struggle in Vietnam only if we recognize it for what it is: part of a vast and continuing struggle in which we have been engaged for more than two decades.

Like most of the conflicts that have plagued the world in recent years, the conflict in Vietnam is a product of the great shifts and changes triggered by the Second World War. Out of the war, two continent-wide powers emerged: the United States and the Soviet Union. The colonial customs through which the nations of Western Europe had governed more than a third of the people of the world were, one by one, dismantled. The Soviet Union under [Josef] Stalin embarked on a reckless course of seeking to extend Communist power. An Iron Curtain was erected to enclose large areas of the globe. At the same time, man was learning to harness the power of the exploding sun, and technology made mockery of time and distance.

The result of these vast changes—compressed within the breathless span of two decades—was to bring about a drastic rearrangement of the power structure of the world.

A Western Dam

This rearrangement of power has resulted in a very uneasy equilibrium of forces. For even while the new national boundaries were still being marked on the map, the Soviet Union under Stalin exploited the confusion to push out the perimeter of its power and influence in an effort to extend the outer limits of Communist domination by force or the threat of force.

This process threatened the freedom of the world. It had to be checked and checked quickly. By launching the Marshall plan to restore economic vitality to the nations of Western Europe and by forming NATO [North Atlantic Treaty Organization]—a powerful Western alliance reinforced by U.S. resources and military power—America and the free nations of Europe built a dam to hold back the further encroachment of Communist ambitions.

This decisive action succeeded brilliantly. NATO, created in 1949, stopped the spread of communism over Western Europe and the northern Mediterranean. But the world was given no time to relax. The victory of the Chinese Communists in that same year posed a new threat of Communist expansion against an Asia in ferment. Just as the Western world had mobilized its resistance against Communist force in Europe, we had to create an effective counterforce in the Far East if Communist domination were not to spread like a lava flow over the whole area.

Balance Maintained

The first test came quickly in Korea. There the United Nations forces—predominantly American—stopped the drive of Communist North Korea, supported by materiel from the Soviet Union. They stopped a vast Chinese army that followed. They brought to a halt the Communist drive to push out the line that had been drawn and to establish Communist control over the whole Korean peninsula.

The Korean war was fought from a central conviction: that the best hope for freedom and security in the world depended on maintaining the integrity of the postwar arrangements. Stability could be achieved only by making sure that the Communist world did not expand by destroying those arrangements by force and threat and thus upsetting the precarious power balance between the two sides of the Iron Curtain.

It was this conviction that led to our firm stand in Korea. It was this conviction that led America, in the years immediately after Korea, to build a barrier around the whole periphery of the Communist world by encouraging the creation of a series of alliances and commitments from the eastern edge of the NATO area to the Pacific.

The SEATO [Southeast Asia Treaty Organization] treaty that was signed in 1954 was part of that barrier, that structure of alliances. It was ratified by the Senate by a vote of 82 to 1.

Under that treaty and its protocol, the United States and other treaty partners gave their joint and several pledges to guarantee existing boundaries—including the line of demarcation between North and South Vietnam established when the French relinquished their control over Indochina. Since then, three Presidents have reinforced that guarantee by further commitments given directly to the Republic of Vietnam. And on August 10, 1964, the Senate, by a vote of 88 to 2, and the House, by a vote of 416 to 0, adopted a joint resolution declaring their support for these commitments. . . .

Subversion Since 1954

Is the war in South Vietnam an external aggression from the north, or is it an indigenous revolt? This is a question that Americans quite properly ask—and one to which they deserve a satisfactory answer. It is a question which we who have official responsibilities have necessarily probed in great depth. For if the Vietnam war were merely what the Communists say it is—an indigenous rebellion—then the United States would have no business taking sides in the conflict and helping one side to defeat the other by force of arms.

The evidence on the character of the Vietnam war is voluminous. Its meaning seems clear enough: The North Vietnamese regime in Hanoi systematically created the Vietcong forces; it provides their equipment; it mounted the guerrilla war—and it controls that war from Hanoi on a day-to-day basis.

The evidence shows clearly enough that—at the time of French withdrawal—when Vietnam was divided in the settlement of 1954, the Communist regime in Hanoi never intended that South Vietnam should develop in freedom. Many Communists fighting with the Vietminh Army were directed to stay in the south, to cache away their arms and to do everything possible to undermine the South Vietnamese Government. Others—80,000 in all—were ordered to the north for training in the North Vietnamese Army.

U.S. troops continued to be sent to Vietnam despite the growing antiwar movement at home.

The evidence is clear enough also that the communist rulers of the north resorted to guerrilla warfare in South Vietnam only when the success of the South Vietnam Government persuaded them that they could not achieve their designs by subversion alone.

In September 1960, the Lao Dong Party—the Communist Party in North Vietnam—held its third party congress in Hanoi. That congress called for the creation of a front organization to undertake the subversion of South Vietnam. Within 2 or 3 months thereafter, the National Liberation Front was established to provide a political facade for the conduct of an active guerrilla war.

Beginning early that year, the Hanoi regime began to infiltrate across the demarcation line the disciplined Communists whom the party had ordered north at the time of the settlement. In the intervening period since 1954, those men had been trained in the arts of proselytizing, sabotage, and subversion. Now they were ordered to conscript young men from the villages by force or persuasion and to form cadres around which guerrilla units could be built. . . .

An Unacceptable Condition

This point is at the heart of our determination to stay the course in the bloody contest now underway in South Vietnam. It also necessarily shapes our position with regard to negotiations.

The President [Lyndon Johnson], Secretary [Dean] Rusk, and all spokesmen for the administration have stated again and again that the United States is prepared to join in unconditional discussions of the Vietnamese problem in an effort to bring about a satisfactory political solution. But so far, the regime in Hanoi has refused to come to the bargaining table except on the basis of quite unacceptable conditions. One among several such conditions—but one that has been widely debated in the United States—is that we must recognize the National Liberation Front as the representative—indeed, as the sole representative—of the South Vietnamese people.

Yet to recognize the National Liberation Front in such a capacity would do violence to the truth and betray the very people whose liberty we are fighting to secure. The National Liberation Front is not a political entity expressing the will of the people of South Vietnam—or any substantial element of the South Vietnamese population. It is a facade fabricated by the Hanoi regime to confuse the issue and elaborate the myth of an indigenous revolt. . . .

Reinforcing a Fiction

To be sure, the Vietcong military forces include a number of indigenous southerners under northern control. Neither the United States nor the South Vietnamese Government has ever questioned that fact. But the composition of the Vietcong military forces is not the issue when one discusses the role of the front. The issue is whether the front has any color of claim as a political entity to represent these indigenous elements.

The evidence makes clear that it does not.

It is purely and simply a fictitious organization created by Hanoi to reinforce a fiction. To recognize it as the representative of the South Vietnamese population would be to give legitimacy to that fiction.

The true party in interest on the enemy side—the entity that has launched the attack on the South Vietnamese Government for its own purposes, the entity that has created, controlled and supplied the fighting forces of the Vietcong from the beginning—is the North Vietnamese regime in Hanoi. And it is the failure of that regime to come to the bargaining table that has so far frustrated every effort to move the problem of South Vietnam from a military to a political solution.

In spite of these clear realities, we have not taken—nor do we take—an obdurate or unreasoning attitude with regard to the front. The President said in his state of the Union message, "We will meet at any conference table, we will discuss any proposal—4 points, or 14 or 40—and we will consider the views of any group"—and that, of course, includes the front along with other groups.

As the President has also said, this false issue of the front would never prove "an insurmountable problem" if Hanoi were prepared for serious negotiations. But we cannot, to advance the political objectives of the Communist regime in Hanoi, give legitimacy to a spurious organization as though it spoke for the people of South Vietnam.

Every Boundary Is Important

A European friend once critically observed that Americans have "a sense of mission but no sense of history." That accusation is, I think, without warrant.

We do have a sense of history and it is that which enables us to view the war in South Vietnam for what it is. We Americans know that it is not, as I have said earlier, a local conflict; it is part of a continuing struggle to prevent the Communists from upsetting the fragile balance of power through force or the threat of force.

To succeed in that struggle, we must resist every Communist effort to destroy by aggression the boundaries and demarcation lines established by the postwar arrangements. We cannot pick and choose among those boundaries. We cannot defend Berlin and yield Korea. We cannot recognize one commitment and repudiate another without tearing and weakening the entire structure on which the world's security depends. . . .

Unfinished Business

This does not mean, however, that the political shape of the world should be regarded as frozen in an intractable pattern; that the boundaries established by the postwar arrangements are necessarily sacrosanct and immutable. Indeed, some of the lines of demarcation drawn after the World War II were explicitly provisional and were to be finally determined in political settlements yet to come. This was true in Germany, in Korea, and South Vietnam as well.

But those settlements have not yet been achieved, and we cannot permit their resolution to be preempted by force. This is the issue in Vietnam. This is what we are fighting for. This is why we are there.

We have no ambition to stay there any longer than is necessary. We have made repeatedly clear that the United States seeks no territory in southeast Asia. We wish no military bases. We do not desire to destroy the regime in Hanoi or to remake it in a Western pattern. The United States will not retain American forces in South Vietnam once peace is assured.

The countries of southeast Asia can be nonalined or neutral, depending on the will of the people. We support free elections in South Vietnam as soon as violence has been eliminated and the South Vietnamese people can vote without intimidation. We look forward to free elections—and we will accept the result as a democratic people is accustomed to do.

Yet we have little doubt about the outcome, for we are confident that the South Vietnamese who have fought hard for their freedom will not be the first people to give up that freedom to communism in a free exercise of self-determination.

Whether the peoples of the two parts of Vietnam will wish to unite is again for them to decide as soon as they are in a position to do so freely. Like other options, that of ramification must be preserved.

A Shared Interest

In the long run, our hopes for the people of South Vietnam reflect our hopes for people everywhere. What we seek is a world living in peace and freedom—a world in which the cold war, with its tensions and conflicts, can recede into history. We are seeking to build a world in which men and nations will recognize and act upon a strongly shared interest in peace and international cooperation for the common good.

We should not despair of these objectives even though at the moment they may seem rather unreal and idealistic. . . .

After all, it is not the American purpose simply to preserve the status quo. That was not our history and that is not our destiny. What we want to preserve is the freedom of choice for the peoples of the world. We will take our chances on that.

The United States Will Defeat the Communist Aggressors

William C. Westmoreland

From 1965 to 1967, U.S. military personnel in Vietnam increased from twenty-three thousand to nearly four hundred thousand troops serving under General William C. Westmoreland, commander of United States Military Assistance Command in Vietnam (MACV). As American participation in the war increased, American participation in antiwar demonstrations also increased. On April 15, 1967, more than one hundred thousand American citizens, including civil rights leader Martin Luther King Jr., demonstrated against the Vietnam War in New York City and in San Francisco.

On April 28, 1967, General Westmoreland responded in the following address to Congress by defending the Johnson administration's position that the United States is not fighting an internal insurrection but is defending the free nation of South Vietnam from external North Vietnamese aggression. He describes the brutal nature of Communist terrorism in South Vietnam, but assures Congress that the current U.S. military strategy is appropriate and that the enemy is becoming demoralized. He expresses his optimism that U.S. troops will prevail with the support of the American people. After hearing Westmoreland's speech and other optimistic military reports about the progress of the war, the American public was shocked

Excerpted from William C. Westmoreland's address before the United States Congress, April 28, 1967.

nine months later when Communist forces mounted a surprise Tet Offensive, which was repelled by American and South Vietnamese forces after nearly a month of intense fighting. The Tet Offensive suggested that the enemy was not demoralized and that military reports had been either deliberately misleading or shockingly mistaken. After President Lyndon Johnson replaced General Westmoreland as commander of U.S. forces in South Vietnam in 1968, Westmoreland complained that Johnson had bullied him into giving speeches to generate support for the war.

I am deeply honored to address the Congress of the United States. I stand in the shadow of military men who have been here before me, but none of them could have had more pride than mine in representing the gallant American fighting men in Vietnam today.

These servicemen and women are sensitive to their mission and, as the record shows, they are unbeatable in carrying out that mission.

As their commander in the field, I have seen many of you in Vietnam during the last 3 years. Without exception, you gentlemen have shown interest, responsibility, and concern for the commitment which we have undertaken, and for the welfare of our troops.

The Republic of Vietnam is fighting to build a strong nation while aggression—organized, directed, and supported from without—attempts to engulf it. This is an unprecedented challenge for a small nation. But it is a challenge which will confront any nation that is marked as a target for the Communist stratagem called war of national liberation.

I can assure you here and now that militarily this strategy will not succeed in Vietnam.

Aggression from the North

In 3 years of close study and daily observation, I have seen no evidence that this is an internal insurrection. I have seen much evidence to the contrary—documented by the enemy himself—that it is aggression from the north.

Since 1954, when the Geneva accord was signed, the North Vietnamese have been sending leaders, political organizers, technicians, and experts on terrorism and sabotage into the south. Clandestinely directed from the north, they and their Hanoi-trained southern counterparts have controlled the entire course of the attack against the Republic of South Vietnam.

More than 2 years ago, North Vietnamese divisions began to arrive, and the control was no longer clandestine. Since then, the buildup of enemy forces has been formidable. During the last 22 months, the number of enemy combat battalions in the south has increased significantly, and nearly half of them are now North Vietnamese. In the same period, overall enemy strength has nearly doubled in spite of large combat losses.

Enemy commanders are skilled professionals. In general, their troops are indoctrinated, well trained, aggressive, and under tight control. . . .

Terrorism

This enemy also uses terror—murder, mutilation, abduction, and the deliberate shelling of innocent men, women, and children—to exercise control through fear. Terror, which he employs daily, is much harder to counter than his best conventional moves.

A typical day in Vietnam was last Sunday. Terrorists near Saigon assassinated a 39-year-old village chief. The same day in the delta they kidnapped 26 civilians, assisting in arranging for local elections. The next day the Vietcong attacked a group of Revolutionary Development workers, killing one and wounding 12 with grenades and machinegun fire in one area, and in another they opened fire on a small civilian bus and killed three and wounded four of its passengers. These are cases of calculated enemy attack on civilians to extend by fear that which they cannot gain by persuasion. One hears little of this brutality here at home. What we do hear about is our own aerial bombing against North Vietnam, and I would like to address this for a moment.

For years the enemy has been blowing bridges, interrupting traffic, cutting roads, sabotaging power stations, blocking canals, and attacking airfields in the south, and he continues to do so. This is a daily occurrence. Bombing in the north has been centered on precisely these same kinds of targets and for the same military purposes—to reduce the supply, interdict the movement, and impair the effectiveness of enemy military forces.

Within his capabilities the enemy in Vietnam is waging total war all day—every day—everywhere. He believes in force, and his intensification of violence is limited only by his resources and not by any moral inhibitions.

To us a cease-fire means "cease-fire." Our observance of past truces has been open and subject to public scrutiny. The enemy permits no such observation in the north or the south. He traditionally has exploited cease-fire periods when the bombing has been suspended to increase his resupply and infiltration activities. This is the enemy—this has been the challenge. The only strategy which can defeat such an organization is one of unrelenting, but discriminating military, political, and psychological pressure on his whole structure—at all levels. From his capabilities and his recent activities, I believe the enemy's probable course of action in the months ahead can be forecast.

In order to carry out his battlefield doctrine I foresee that he will continue his buildup across the demilitarized zone and through Laos, and he will attack when he believes he has a chance for a dramatic blow. He will not return exclusively to guerrilla warfare, although he certainly will continue to intensify his guerrilla activities.

I expect the enemy to continue to increase his mortar, artillery, rocket, and recoilless rifle attacks on our installations. At the same time, he will step up his attacks on villages and district towns to intimidate the people, and to thwart the democratic processes now underway in South Vietnam.

Given the nature of the enemy, it seems to me that the strategy that we are following at this time is the proper one, and that it is producing results. While he obviously is far from quitting, there are signs that his morale and his military structure are beginning to deteriorate. The rate of decline will be in proportion to the pressure directed against him. . . .

Support from Home

Our President [Lyndon B. Johnson] and the representatives of the people of the United States, the Congress, have seen to it that our troops in the field have been well supplied and equipped. When a field commander does not have to look over his shoulder to see whether he is being supported, he can concentrate on the battlefield with much greater assurance of success. I speak for my troops, when I say we are thankful for this unprecedented material support.

As I have said before, in evaluating the enemy strategy it is evident to me that he believes our Achilles' heel is our resolve. Your continued strong support is vital to the success of our mission.

Our soldiers, sailors, airmen, marines, and coastguardsmen in Vietnam are the finest ever fielded by our Nation. In this assessment I include Americans of all races, creeds, and colors. Your servicemen in Vietnam are intelligent, skilled, dedicated, and courageous. In these qualities no unit, no service, no ethnic group, and no national origin can claim priority.

These men understand the conflict and their complex roles as fighters and as builders. They believe in what they are doing. They are determined to provide the shield of security behind which the Republic of Vietnam can develop and prosper for its own sake and for the future and freedom of all Southeast Asia.

Backed at home by resolve, confidence, patience, determination, and continued support, we will prevail in Vietnam over the Communist aggressor. . . .

The United States Must Fight with Limited Means for Limited Objectives

Dean Rusk

As United States secretary of state for eight years under Presidents John F. Kennedy and Lyndon B. Johnson, Dean Rusk had a key role in shaping American foreign policy in Southeast Asia and in advising President Johnson on the conduct of the Vietnam War. By late 1967, the number of U.S. troops in Vietnam was approaching five hundred thousand soldiers. As antiwar protest escalated in parallel with Johnson's escalation of American involvement, Rusk began speaking in support of the war.

Responding to the "current public discussion of Vietnam" at a news conference in Washington, D.C., on October 12, 1967, just four days before nationwide antiwar demonstrations, Secretary Rusk addresses two diametrically opposed antiwar positions: that American forces should immediately withdraw and that American forces should use all available means to win the war quickly and decisively. Citing the SEATO (Southeast Asian Treaty Organization) Treaty of 1954 and the Gulf of Tonkin Resolution in August 1964, Dean argues that the United States has committed to the defense of South Vietnam and that an immediate American withdrawal would lead adversaries to think that U.S. commitments are bluffs. On the other hand, Rusk urges Americans to be patient with limited warfare, arguing that fighting with limited means for

Excerpted from Dean Rusk's news conference, October 12, 1967.

limited objectives is necessary to avoid total catastrophe. In closing, he expresses his optimism about progress toward peace in South Vietnam. Rusk later claimed to have opposed Kennedy's introduction of U.S. military personnel into South Vietnam and Johnson's escalation of the war.

I should like to begin with a brief comment on the current public discussion of Vietnam.

I find no significant body of American opinion which would have us withdraw from Vietnam and abandon Southeast Asia to the fate which Asian communism has planned for it. Similarly, I find no serious opinion among us which wishes to transform this struggle into a general war.

We Americans are, therefore, debating variations on a theme—but the theme is a central position resting upon (a) the need to meet our commitments and defend our vital national interests; (b) the pursuit of our limited objectives by limited means, and (c) our earnest desire to bring this conflict to a peaceful conclusion as soon as possible. Hanoi particularly should not misunderstand the character of this debate.

Our commitment is clear and our national interest is real. The SEATO [Southeast Asia Treaty Organization] Treaty approved with only one dissenting vote by our Senate, declares that "Each party recognizes that aggression by means of armed attack in the treaty area . . . would endanger its own peace and safety, and agrees that it will in that event act to meet the common danger . . ."

The Treaty says "each party" will act. The fidelity of the United States is not subject to the veto of some other signatory—and five signatories have engaged their forces alongside Korean and South Vietnamese troops. Indeed, the proportion of non-U.S. forces in South Vietnam is greater than non-U.S. forces in Korea.

In August, 1964, the Congress by joint resolution declared, with only two dissenting votes, that "The United States regards as vital to its national interest and to world peace the maintenance of international peace and security in Southeast Asia." This was not a new idea in 1964. It was the basis for the SEATO Treaty a decade earlier. It is no less valid in 1967. Our several alliances in the Pacific reflect our profound interest in peace in the Pacific, and in Asia where two-thirds of the world's people live, no less vital to us as a Nation than is peace in our own hemisphere or in the [North Atlantic Treaty Organization] area.

I have heard the word "credibility" injected into our domestic debate. Let me say, as solemnly as I can, that those who would place in question the credibility of the pledged word of the United States under our mutual security treaties would subject this Nation to mortal danger. If any who would be our adversary should suppose that our treaties are a bluff or will be abandoned if the going gets tough, the result could be catastrophe for all mankind.

It is not easy for our people to wage a struggle by limited means for limited objectives. We Americans are an impatient people—a quality which has helped to build a great Nation. The present impatience about Vietnam is thoroughly understandable—and is shared by those who carry official responsibility. But our overriding object is—and must be in this modern world—the establishment of a reliable peace. It is easy to rush into total catastrophe. It requires courage and determination to act with both firmness and restraint in the interest of peace. An examination of the crises in which we have been involved since 1945 will show, I think, the supremacy of the objective of a reliable peace.

President [Lyndon B.] Johnson has emphasized, time and time again, his interest in a prompt and peaceful settlement of the present struggles in Southeast Asia. Just two weeks ago, in San Antonio, he said:

"The United States is willing to stop all aerial and naval bombardment of North Vietnam when this will lead promptly to productive discussions. We, of course, assume that while discussions proceed, North Vietnam would not take advantage of the bombing cessation or limitation."

Can there be a more reasonable proposal? Is there anything unfair about such a simple proposition? Is it not clear that if Hanoi is interested in peace it could say "yes" publicly or privately to the President's offer?

A rejection, or a refusal even to discuss such a formula for peace, requires that we face some sober conclusions. It would mean that Hanoi has not abandoned its effort to seize South Vietnam by force. It would give reality and credibility to captured documents which describe a "fight and negotiate" strategy by Vietcong and the North Vietnamese forces. It would reflect a view in Hanoi that they can gamble upon the character of the American people and of our allies in the Pacific.

Earlier I referred to variations on a theme. The debate in which we are now involved is essentially a debate above detail—this or that military move, this or that diplomatic step, this or that formulation of what is in fact a common middle position. If that be true, precision is important. People at least should make it clear whether they are arguing with Washington or with Hanoi.

When people talk about a pause in the bombing, they should know that Hanoi calls a pause an "ultimatum." When a Senator says that he wants to stop the bombing but, of course, wishes to continue to bomb in support of our Marines south of the DMZ [Demilitarized Zone], he should know that Hanoi categorically rejects any such notion. When people say "Negotiate now," they should know that the President would meet with Ho Chi Minh and other chiefs of state concerned tomorrow—and that I would depart today for any mutually convenient spot if I could meet a representative of North Vietnam with whom I could discuss peace in Southeast Asia.

Chairman [Nguyen Van] Thieu and Prime Minister [Nguyen Cao] Ky have repeatedly offered to meet with the authorities of Hanoi to arrange a cease-fire and a peaceful settlement. They and we both responded affirmatively to [United Nations Secretary General] U Thant's proposals of last March. Had there been a similar response from Hanoi, there would have been discussions to arrange a military standstill, preliminary conversations and a convening of the Geneva conference. Literally dozens of proposals made by ourselves, other governments or groups of governments have been rejected by Hanoi.

I cannot tell you when peace will come. I am encouraged by progress toward peace in South Vietnam, but I cannot name a date. But we shall continue our effort both by resisting those who would impose their solutions by brute force and by an unremitting exploration of every path which could lead to peace.

The United States Must Fight to Win the Vietnam War

Barry Goldwater

As a five-term U.S. senator, Arizona Republican Barry Goldwater had a reputation for staunch conservatism and strong anti-Communist sentiments. In the 1964 presidential campaign, his statement that "extremism in the defense of liberty is no vice" created a public perception of Goldwater as a dangerous extremist, and he lost the election to Lyndon B. Johnson by a landslide. Nevertheless, he continued to call for a more aggressive military effort in Vietnam, criticizing the Johnson administration's policy of limited warfare as weak, ineffectual, and dishonest.

In the following address before his Republican Party colleagues on October 28, 1967, Goldwater claims that the United States is obligated to defend South Vietnam against Communist aggression as a matter of self-defense and therefore cannot withdraw. Because the United States is asking Americans to risk the lives of their sons and because the Vietnam War is a war against violence for all free nations, he proclaims, the United States must fight and must fight to win.

Many years after the end of the Vietnam War, Americans would still debate whether the United States would have won the war with more aggressive tactics and weapons, such as invading North Vietnam or using atomic weapons, or whether such a strategy would have created war with China or the Soviet Union, another world war, or a nuclear catastrophe.

Excerpted from Barry Goldwater's address at the Republican Western Conference, October 28, 1967.

L et me warn you of something at the outset. I am one
Republican, one American who is sick and tired of
hearing the enemies of his country glorified, while the
motives of his country are derided and doubted.

I am one Republican, one American who is tired of hearing defeat defended and victory rejected; of hearing American soldiers villified while rioters are extolled.

I am, finally, one Republican, one American who is tired,
sick and tired of hearing big men play little games with a war
that is costing lives every minute—a real war on a real battlefield, not some chess game in a cloister, not some debater's
point on a platform.

Let me also make it clear. I have not signed a blank check
on my conscience about the war in Vietnam. There are points
of profound disagreement about the way in which it has been
waged, the way it has been defended, the way it has been reported by the President [Lyndon B. Johnson].

I am one Republican, one American who is appalled that
the mothers and fathers of this Nation are asked to send their
most valuable possession—their sons and heirs—to fight half
way around the world with the knowledge that their boys are
not receiving the total backing of their country; that even as
these boys are bleeding and dying the President and his Secretary of Defense [Robert McNamara] are attempting to
wage a war by consensus; are imposing on our fighting men
impossible restrictions and unrealistic objectives.

If the President has the right to ask our military men to
risk their lives on foreign soil he has the corresponding duty
to see that these same men receive a full measure of aid and
assistance not only in military hardware, but in the essential
yet intangible psychological support.

Let us not forget that the American boys in Vietnam and
their parents at home—are making the greatest sacrifice that
any country can extract from its citizens and let us also not
forget that right now these parents have justifiable doubts as
to whether they are receiving their full measure of support
from their President.

Yes, there is no doubt that there is a credibility gap.
There is no doubt that there are even doubts about the terms
on which this administration will or will not end the fighting,

or sign the peace, or go to the conference table. Yes, there is confusion. Yes, there is honest disagreement. Yes, there is responsible dissent. Yes, there is need for all of this.

But *no*, and let me repeat it, *no*, there is no way to avoid the basic facts. We *are* at war. We have the choice between winning and losing. We cannot end the war in any other way. We will either win or we will lose—and all of the sophisticated arguments and tongue-twisting, mind-bending haggling in the world won't change reality.

Reality exists. The war exists. Our stake in it exists. We are there. The enemy is there. We cannot turn off the future in which we or they will emerge with what we want.

War is that moment in a nation's life when it stands face to face with the facts of its own survival. There are no little wars and no big wars. There are just *war* wars; conflicts in which man's most basic possession, his life, is put into the scales. Some may say that there *are* little wars. But no life lost in a little war is a *little* life. Nor can we measure war by the arithmetic of dying. We can measure it only by the mathematics of our morality as a nation. In our case the figures are clear. We have yet to fight a war for gain or conquest. We have fought always in self-defense to further freedom and defend it. We are doing that today.

If this war that we fight is just a little war, whose outcome may be bargained by little deals, then we are a little nation, not a great one.

If this war that we fight today is an aggressive war, and not fought in self-defense, then we are wrong, we are vicious, and we would deserve to be defeated.

By every single objective measure, however, we are fighting in our self-defense. We are not immoral. We are not wrong. We do not deserve defeat and our enemies do not deserve the victory for which so many friends of the Vietcong weep, wail, march and work. . . .

The War Against War

Exactly what, against the background, are the facts involved in Vietnam that transcend completely all partisan politics? The facts involved are the harsh facts of war as an instrument of policy—a tragic, horrible instrument of policy and yet one with which we must deal realistically in the world as it actually exists.

It would not be too far-fetched to say that unless we do understand these facts we can never win the war which all men of good will eagerly fight—the war against war itself.

I have referred many times to one of these facts as the fact of national honor. Let me define it so that there can be no misunderstanding. I do not mean in any sense, just a matter of pride or what some call "face."

Those who try to distort our position in Vietnam by saying we are simply trying to save face, and add that the cost is not worth it, shamefully distort the facts.

National honor in this instance means nothing less than our ability to live up to certain international contracts which we have signed—for our own very enlightened self-interest.

Those contracts are the mutual defense treaties which today bind us to more than three dozen nations around the world.

Goldwater believed the United States was obligated to defend South Vietnam against the Communists.

Without those treaties, communism would be tempted around the globe to escalate its adventures far beyond anything we have seen so far. It is these mutual security treaties which spell out to communism the will of all those who have signed them to resist aggression, to resist force with force if need be.

Tyrants and aggressors understand no language better than this!

One such treaty and promises have bound us to the defense of South Vietnam. Three American Presidents have taken steps to make good on our pledges there. Our involvement in Vietnam is an American involvement; not a partisan involvement.

Should we pull out of Vietnam, leaving it defenseless, or should we have failed to respond to its plight in the first place, we would have pulled the rug out from beneath the security of the entire free world.

Who would yank that rug now? I know that today we hear cries of concern from some of the very nations with whom we are joined in those defense treaties. I cannot help but wonder, however, how much louder would be those cries of concern—and how much more heartfelt—if we suddenly renounced our role in the world, our partnership in security, and turned tail in Vietnam to dig ourselves into an isolated America.

Our mutual security agreements must mean exactly what they say or they would mean nothing at all. And what they say simply is that an attack against any one nation shall be considered an attack against all or, in most practical terms, as an attack against us.

Under these treaties, in effect, *and necessarily*, any one of the nations involved can call us to *instant war* if attacked. Harsh as it sounds, there is no better way to assure peace. An aggressive enemy is never appeased by slow reactions to his ambitions. Instead, such slowness of reaction just breeds new recklessness and new perils.

Three Presidents, a Republican and two Democrats, have reacted point for point to the enemy's actions in Vietnam. The enemy has chosen, point by point, to go ahead. Does this mean that the policy of opposing him has failed? It does not and it has not.

First, the enemy has been stopped from a key conquest. Second, while he has been stopped in Vietnam he actually has been hurled back and out in Indonesia—a major success for the friends of freedom. A major success which, it seems to me, would have been altogether impossible had not our show of strength in Vietnam been underway at the same time.

If the policy in Vietnam has left anything to be desired—
and I am one who agrees that it has—it has been that it has
not been firm *enough* and fast *enough* and honest *enough*. It
has, too often, held out to the enemy false hopes of our
weakening and thus has encouraged him.

Today, all who see horror in Vietnam, and would turn
their eyes from it, also must shut their eyes to the horrors to
come should we get out by giving up.

It is not too much, I feel, to hope that Vietnam will, when
we have won, represent more than a milestone of mutual
security.

It may well represent a watershed of new hope for a
world purged of violence between nations.

For, deeply involved in Vietnam is, at last, the free world's
recognition that when violence is substituted for political
process—no matter the disguise—that men who treasure
peace must march to war.

This is the entire key to our involvement there. It is the
deepest meaning of the concept of mutual security. It is the
deep awareness that aggression in these times no longer parades only under the banners of regular armies marching
across regular battlefields.

Violence Must Be Opposed

Aggression can take many forms and, of course, so may the
defense against it.

The economic aggression of politically priced and aimed
marketing is one form—and the greatest merchant nation on
our earth surely should be able to counter that and even
counter-attack.

The political aggression of international pressure and internal subversion is another form—and surely this Nation,
with its unbroken record of freeing, rather than enslaving
people should be able to counter that, and even counter-attack.

The psychological aggression of chanted slogans and
slanted viewpoints is another form—and surely this Nation,
with the world's most exciting story of progress and prosperity should be able to counter that and even counter-attack.

But when it comes to violence, let me remind you, there

often is no time for the weapons of those other forms. When murder became the Vietcong substitute for reason in Vietnam it became a question of immediate self-defense at the most basic level.

Thus, beyond everything else, what we are saying by our deeds in Vietnam—what we are saying with our lives in Vietnam—is that we will *not* stand by, no matter the time or the place, when violence is thrust upon a friend and when violence is substituted for political process.

The day we seek is the day when no man's hand will be raised against another, when violence will be rejected everywhere as a substitute for reason.

Until that day, we can no more tolerate violence in the affairs of nations than we can tolerate violence in the affairs of our own people.

In self-defense, violence must be opposed. Thugs, whether international or in your neighborhood, cannot be given a license to murder. They will use it. Those who initiate violence anywhere must be stopped—even if they must be stopped violently.

That is what, at the root, Vietnam is about. That is why those who say that we should turn back do not seem to have the haziest notion of why we have gone ahead. They speak of everything but they do not speak of the most important thing—the fact that it was not we, but the enemy who substituted violence for the processes of peace in Vietnam.

It is that very use of violence that is being tested today. Should the cause of violence win, then, of course, days of new violence would dawn everywhere. Violence proven in Vietnam would be violence made useful everywhere.

By the same token, violence beaten back in Vietnam, violence deprived of reward and sanction, violence deprived even of sanctuary, would mean second thoughts about violence everywhere. Yes; even here at home.

If peace is to be won in this world, it must be won from those who threaten it and violently shatter it.

We seek such a victory in Vietnam; a victory over violence itself.

Let no Republican, let no American ever seek less.

GREAT
SPEECHES
IN
HISTORY

The War
at Home

U.S. Corporate Liberalism Creates and Sustains the Vietnam War

Carl Oglesby

Starting in early 1965, antiwar groups, led almost exclusively by students but including professors, religious pacifists, and other citizens, emerged on American university and college campuses. At teach-ins, gatherings to discuss the issues of the Vietnam War, many young Americans questioned U.S. policies and American values that led to American military intervention in Vietnam in violation of the Geneva Accords and to American support of corrupt colonial governments in South Vietnam.

Carl Oglesby was working as an editor for Bendix Aviation, a defense contractor in Ann Arbor, Michigan, when he began writing and publishing essays that criticized U.S. foreign policy in Southeast Asia. After members of the Students for a Democratic Society (SDS), a national student-led political organization, read Oglesby's paper comparing U.S. policy in China with U.S. policy in Vietnam, several members found him and invited his participation. In early 1965, Oglesby joined the SDS, participating in the first teach-in on the University of Michigan campus. In a few months, Oglesby began touring the country and speaking against the war as the new SDS president.

In the following address before protesters in Washington, D.C., Carl Oglesby suggests that the war in Vietnam is an economic war with economic objectives. He argues that

Excerpted from Carl Oglesby's speech at March on Washington, November 27, 1965. Copyright © 1965 by Carl Oglesby. Reprinted with permission.

liberal American leaders have contrived an anti-Communist ideology as a justification for safeguarding American corporate economic interests around the world against revolutionary change. He compares the American Revolutionary War with the Vietnam War and concludes that the National Liberation Front is fighting a revolutionary war in Vietnam. He indicts corporate liberalism for abandoning humanist values and calls for a humanist reformation.

By indicting conflicted American values as the root causes of the Vietnam War, Oglesby's piercing economic analysis created a philosophical foundation for the antiwar movement, influenced antiwar leaders and congressmen, stimulated the development of countercultural values in a generation of Americans, and anticipated U.S. foreign policy decisions in support of corporate interests during the years following the war for the remainder of the century.

S even months ago at the April March on Washington, Paul Potter, then President of Students for a Democratic Society, stood in approximately this spot and said that we must name the system that creates and sustains the war in Vietnam—name it, describe it, analyze it, understand it, and change it.

Today I will try to name it—to suggest an analysis which, to be quite frank, may disturb some of you—and to suggest what changing it may require of us.

We are here again to protest a growing war. Since it is a very bad war, we acquire the habit of thinking it must be caused by very bad men. But we only conceal reality, I think, to denounce on such grounds the menacing coalition of industrial and military power, or the brutality of the blitzkrieg we are waging against Vietnam, or the ominous signs around us that heresy may soon no longer be permitted. We must simply observe, and quite plainly say, that this coalition, this blitzkrieg, and this demand for acquiescence are creatures, all of them, of a Government that since 1932 has considered itself to be fundamentally liberal.

The original commitment in Vietnam was made by President [Harry S.] Truman, a mainstream liberal. It was seconded by President [Dwight D.] Eisenhower, a moderate liberal. It was intensified by the late President [John F.] Kennedy, a flaming liberal. Think of the men who now engineer that war—those who study the maps, give the commands, push the buttons, and tally the dead: [McGeorge] Bundy, [Robert] McNamara, [Dean] Rusk, [Henry Cabot] Lodge, [Arthur] Goldberg, the President himself. They are not moral monsters. They are all honorable men. They are all liberals.

But so, I'm sure, are many of us who are here today in protest. To understand the war, then, it seems necessary to take a closer look at this American liberalism. Maybe we are in for some surprises. Maybe we have here two quite different liberalisms: one authentically humanist; the other not so human at all.

Not long ago I considered myself a liberal and if, someone had asked me what I meant by that, I'd perhaps have quoted Thomas Jefferson or Thomas Paine, who first made plain our nation's unprovisional commitment to human rights. But what do you think would happen if these two heroes could sit down now for a chat with President [Lyndon] Johnson and McGeorge Bundy?

They would surely talk of the Vietnam war. Our dead revolutionaries would soon wonder why their country was fighting against what appeared to be a revolution. The living liberals would hotly deny that it is one: there are troops coming in from outside, the rebels get arms from other countries, most of the people are not on their side, and they practice terror against their own. Therefore: not a revolution.

What would our dead revolutionaries answer? They might say: "What fools and bandits, sirs, you make then of us. Outside help? Do you remember Lafayette? Or the three thousand British freighters the French navy sunk for our side? Or the arms and men, we got from France and Spain? And what's this about terror? Did you never hear what we did to our own Loyalists? Or about the thousands of rich American Tories who fled for their lives to Canada? And as for popular support, do you not know that we had less than one-third of our people with us? That, in fact, the colony of

New York recruited more troops for the British than for the revolution? Should we give it all back?"

The Revolution in Vietnam

Revolutions do not take place in velvet boxes. They never have. It is only the poets who make them lovely. What the National Liberation Front is fighting in Vietnam is a complex and vicious war. This war is also a revolution, as honest a revolution as you can find anywhere in history. And this is a fact which all our intricate official denials will never change.

But it doesn't make any difference to our leaders anyway. Their aim in Vietnam is really much simpler than this implies. It is to safeguard what they take to be American interests around the world against revolution or revolutionary change, which they always call Communism—as if that were that. In the case of Vietnam, this interest is, first, the principle that revolution shall not be tolerated anywhere, and second, that South Vietnam shall never sell its rice to China—or even to North Vietnam.

There is simply no such thing now, for us, as a just revolution—never mind that for two-thirds of the world's people the Twentieth Century might as well be the Stone Age; never mind the melting poverty and hopelessness that are the basic facts of life for most modern men; and never mind that for these millions there is now an increasingly perceptible relationship between their sorrow and our contentment.

Can we understand why the Negroes of Watts rebelled? Then why do we need a devil theory to explain the rebellion of the South Vietnamese? Can we understand the oppression in Mississippi, or the anguish that our Northern ghettoes makes epidemic? Then why can't we see that our proper human struggle is not with Communism or revolutionaries, but with the social desperation that drives good men to violence, both here and abroad?

To be sure, we have been most generous with our aid, and in Western Europe, a mature industrial society, that aid worked. But there are always political and financial strings. And we have never shown ourselves capable of allowing others to make those traumatic institutional changes that are often the prerequisites of progress in colonial societies. For all our official feeling for the millions who are enslaved to what we so self-righteously call the yoke of Communist tyranny, we make no real effort at all to crack through the much more vicious right-wing tyrannies that our businessmen traffic with and our nation profits from every day. And for all our cries about the international Red conspiracy to take over the world, we take only pride in the fact of our six thousand military bases on foreign soil. . . .

A Nation of Beardless Liberals

We are saddened and puzzled by random backpage stories of revolt in this or that Latin American state—but are convinced by a few pretty photos in the Sunday supplement that things are getting better, that the world is coming our way, that change from disorder can be orderly, that our benevolence will pacify the distressed, that our might will intimidate the angry.

Optimists, may I suggest that these are quite unlikely fantasies? They are fantasies because we have lost that mysterious social desire for human equity that from time to time has given us genuine moral drive. We have become a nation of young, bright-eyed, hard-hearted, slim-waisted, bullet-headed make-out artists. A nation—may I say it?—of beardless liberals.

You say I am being hard? Only think.

This country, with its thirty-some years of liberalism can send 200,000 young men to Vietnam to kill and die in the most dubious of wars, but it cannot get 100 voter registrars to go into Mississippi.

What do you make of it?

The financial burden of the war obliges us to cut millions from an already pathetic War on Poverty budget. But in almost the same breath, Congress appropriates one hundred forty million dollars for the Lockheed and Boeing companies to compete with each other on the supersonic transport project—that Disneyland creation that will cost us all about two billion dollars before it's done.

What do you make of it?

Many of us have been earnestly resisting for some years now the idea of putting atomic weapons into West German hands, an action that would perpetuate the division of Europe and thus the Cold War. Now just this week we find out that, with the meagerest of security systems, West Germany has had nuclear weapons in her hands for the past six years.

What do you make of it?

Some will make of it that I overdraw the matter. Many will ask: What about the other side? To be sure, there is the bitter ugliness of Czechoslovakia, Poland, those infamous Russian tanks in the streets of Budapest. But my anger only rises to hear some say that sorrow cancels sorrow, or that this one's shame deposits in that one's account the right to shamefulness.

And others will make of it that I sound mighty anti-American. To these, I say: Don't blame me for that! Blame those who mouthed my liberal values and broke my American heart. . . .

Our American Corporate System

We do not say these men are evil. We say, rather, that good men can be divided from their compassion by the institutional system that inherits us all. Generation in and out, we are put to use. People become instruments. Generals do not hear the screams of the bombed; sugar executives do not see the misery of the cane cutters: for to do so is to be that much less the general, that much less the executive.

The foregoing facts of recent history describe one main aspect of the estate of Western liberalism. Where is our American humanism here? What went wrong?

Let's stare our situation coldly in the face. All of us are born to the colossus of history, our American corporate system—in many ways an awesome organism. There is one fact that describes it: With about five per cent of the world's people, we consume about half the world's goods. We take a richness that is in good part not our own, and we put it in our pockets, our garages, our split-levels, our bellies, and our futures.

On the *face* of it, it is a crime that so few should have so much at the expense of so many. Where is the moral imagination so abused as to call this just? Perhaps many of us feel a bit uneasy in our sleep. We are not, after all, a cruel people. And perhaps we don't really need this super-dominance that deforms others. But what can we do? The investments are made. The financial ties are established. The plants abroad are built. Our system exists. One is swept up into it. How intolerable—to be born moral, but addicted to a stolen and maybe surplus luxury. Our goodness threatens to become counterfeit before our eyes—unless we change. But change threatens us with uncertainty—at least.

Our problem, then, is to justify this system and give its theft another name—to make kind and moral what is neither, to perform some alchemy with language that will make this injustice seem a most magnanimous gift.

A hard problem. But the Western democracies, in the heyday of their colonial expansionism, produced a hero worthy of the task.

Its name was free enterprise, and its partner was an *illiberal liberalism* that said to the poor and the dispossessed: What we acquire of your resources we repay in civilization: the white man's burden. But this was too poetic. So a much more hardheaded theory was produced. This theory said that colonial status is in fact a *boon* to the colonized. We give them technology and bring them into modern times.

But this deceived no one but ourselves. We were delighted with this new theory. The poor saw in it merely an admission that their claims were irrefutable. They stood up to us, without gratitude. We were shocked—but also confused, for the poor seemed again to be right. How long is it going to be the case, we wondered, that the poor will be right and the rich will be wrong?

Liberalism faced a crisis. In the face of the collapse of the European empires, how could it continue, to hold together, our twin need for richness and righteousness? How can we continue to sack the ports of Asia and still dream of Jesus?

The Ideology of Anti-Communism

The challenge was met with a most ingenious solution: the ideology of anti-Communism. This was the bind: we cannot call revolution bad, because we started that way ourselves, and because it is all too easy to see why the dispossessed should rebel. So we will call revolution Communism. And we will reserve for ourselves the right to say what Communism means. We take note of revolution's enormities, wrenching them where necessary from their historical context and often exaggerating them, and say: Behold, Communism is a bloodbath. We take note of those reactionaries who stole the revolution, and say: Behold, Communism is a betrayal of the people. We take note of the revolution's need to consolidate itself, and say: Behold, Communism is a tyranny.

It has been all these things, and it will be these things again, and we will never be at a loss for those tales of atrocity that comfort us so in our self-righteousness. Nuns will be raped and bureaucrats will be disembowelled. Indeed, revolution is a *fury*. For it is a letting loose of outrages pent up sometimes over centuries. But the more brutal and longer-lasting the suppression of this energy, all the more ferocious will be its explosive release.

Far from helping Americans deal with this truth, the anti-Communist ideology merely tries to disguise it so that things may stay the way they are. Thus, it depicts our presence in other lands not as a coercion, but a protection. It allows us even to say that the napalm in Vietnam is only another aspect of our humanitarian love—like those exorcisms in the Middle Ages that so often killed the patient. So we say to the Vietnamese peasant, the Cuban intellectual, the Peruvian worker: "You are better dead than Red. If it hurts or if you don't understand why—sorry about that."

This is the action of *corporate liberalism*. It performs for the corporate state a function quite like what the Church once performed for the feudal state. It seeks to justify its burdens and protect it from change. As the Church exaggerated this office in the Inquisition, so with liberalism in the [Senator Joseph] McCarthy time—which, if it was a reactionary phenomenon, was still made possible by our anti-communist corporate liberalism.

Let me then speak directly to humanist liberals. If my facts are wrong, I will soon be corrected. But if they are right, then you may face a crisis of conscience. Corporatism or humanism: which? For it has come to that. Will you let your dreams be used? Will you be a grudging apologist for the corporate state? Or will you help try to change it—not in the name of this or that blueprint or ism, but in the name of simple human decency and democracy and the vision that wise and brave men saw in the time of our own Revolution?

And if your commitment to human values is unconditional, then disabuse yourselves of the notion that statements will bring change, if only the right statements can be written, or that interviews with the mighty will bring change if only the mighty can be reached, or that marches will bring change if only we can make them massive enough, or that policy proposals will bring change if only we can make them responsible enough.

We are dealing now with a colossus that does not want to be changed. It will not change itself. It will not cooperate with those who want to change it. Those allies of ours in the Government—are they *really* our allies? If they *are*, then they don't need advice, they need *constituencies*; they don't need study groups, they need a *movement*. And if they are *not*, then all the more reason for building that movement with the most relentless conviction.

There are people in this country today who are trying to build that movement, who aim at nothing less than a humanist reformation. And the humanist liberals must understand that it is this movement with which their own best hopes are most in tune. We radicals know the same history that you liberals know, and we can understand your occasional cynicism, exasperation, and even distrust. But we ask you to put these aside and help us risk a leap. Help us find enough time for the enormous work that needs doing here. Help us build. Help us shape the future in the name of plain human hope.

The Vietnam War Is a Symptom of an American Spiritual Malady

Martin Luther King Jr.

As president of the Southern Christian Leadership Conference from 1957 until his assassination in 1968, Dr. Martin Luther King Jr. was a pivotal figure in the Civil Rights Movement. On thirty occasions King demonstrated his moral integrity by going to jail for his values. In recognition of his dedication to nonviolent direct action for peace and social justice, King was awarded the Nobel Peace Prize in 1964.

King had hesitated to speak against the Vietnam War, fearing that his opposition would divert energy from the civil rights movement. By 1967, however, he realized that the war was already diverting energy from civil rights issues, and he decided to break the silence. Speaking at the Riverside Church in New York City on the evening of April 4, 1967, exactly one year before his assassination in Memphis, Tennessee, King urges members of Clergy and Laymen Concerned About Vietnam to join him in protesting the madness of the war. Among his reasons for opposing the war, King suggests that the expense of the war is crippling social programs at home and that minority men are fighting and dying in disproportionate numbers for liberties that they do not have at home. By viewing American policies from the perspective of the

Vietnamese people, King exposes the hypocrisy of thinking Americans are liberators in Vietnam, and he pleads,
"Somehow this madness must cease." Citing profit motives, property rights, racism, extreme materialism, and
militarism as values indicating an American spiritual ill-
ness, King calls for a revolution in values, a shift toward
loyalty to mankind as a whole, to get America on the
right side of world revolution.

By casting the Vietnam War as a civil rights issue,
King legitimated the antiwar movement for minorities,
bringing large numbers of minority activists into antiwar
demonstrations and fueling growing antiwar sentiment.
In addition, King's moral analysis of the war galvanized
antiwar actions by religious leaders and their congrega-
tions and undermined justifications for war by government officials.

I come to this magnificent house of worship tonight because my conscience leaves me no other choice. I join
you in this meeting because I am in deepest agreement
with the aims and work of the organization which has
brought us together, Clergy and Laymen Concerned About
Vietnam. The recent statements of your executive committee
are the sentiments of my own heart, and I found myself in
full accord when I read its opening lines: "A time comes
when silence is betrayal." That time has come for us in relation to Vietnam.

The truth of these words is beyond doubt, but the mission to which they call us is a most difficult one. Even when
pressed by the demands of inner truth, men do not easily assume the task of opposing their government's policy, especially in time of war. Nor does the human spirit move without great difficulty against all the apathy of conformist
thought within one's own bosom and in the surrounding
world. Moreover, when the issues at hand seem as perplex-
ing as they often do in the case of this dreadful conflict, we
are always on the verge of being mesmerized by uncertainty.
But we must move on. . . .

A Moral Vision of Vietnam

Since I am a preacher by calling, I suppose it is not surprising that I have seven major reasons for bringing Vietnam into the field of my moral vision. There is at the outset a very obvious and almost facile connection between the war in Vietnam and the struggle I and others have been waging in America. A few years ago there was a shining moment in that struggle. It seemed as if there was a real promise of hope for the poor, both black and white, through the poverty program. There were experiments, hopes, new beginnings. Then came the buildup in Vietnam, and I watched this program broken and eviscerated as if it were some idle political plaything of a society gone mad on war. And I knew that America would never invest the necessary funds or energies in rehabilitation of its poor so long as adventures like Vietnam continued to draw men and skills and money like some demonic, destructive suction tube. So I was increasingly compelled to see the war as an enemy of the poor and to attack it as such.

Perhaps a more tragic recognition of reality took place when it became clear to me that the war was doing far more than devastating the hopes of the poor at home. It was sending their sons and their brothers and their husbands to fight and to die in extraordinarily high proportions relative to the rest of the population. We were taking the black young men who had been crippled by our society and sending them eight thousand miles away to guarantee liberties in Southeast Asia which they had not found in southwest Georgia and East Harlem. So we have been repeatedly faced with the cruel irony of watching Negro and white boys on TV screens as they kill and die together for a nation that has been unable to seat them together in the same schools. So we watch them in brutal solidarity burning the huts of a poor village, but we realize that they would hardly live on the same block in Chicago. I could not be silent in the face of such cruel manipulation of the poor.

My third reason moves to an even deeper level of awareness, for it grows out of my experience in the ghettos of the North over the last three years, especially the last three summers. As I have walked among the desperate, rejected, and angry young men, I have told them that Molotov cocktails and rifles would not solve their problems. I have tried to offer them my deepest compassion while maintaining my conviction that social change comes most meaningfully through nonviolent action. But they asked, and rightly so, "What about Vietnam?" They asked if our own nation wasn't using massive doses of violence to solve its problems, to bring about the changes it wanted. Their questions hit home, and I knew that I could never again raise my voice against the violence of the oppressed in the ghettos without having first spoken clearly to the greatest purveyor of violence in the world today: my own government. For the sake of those boys, for the sake of this government, for the sake of the hundreds of thousands trembling under our violence, I cannot be silent.

For those who ask the question, "Aren't you a civil rights leader?" and thereby mean to exclude me from the movement for peace, I have this further answer. In 1957, when a group of us formed the Southern Christian Leadership Conference, we chose as our motto: "To save the soul of America.". . .

Now it should be incandescently clear that no one who has any concern for the integrity and life of America today can ignore the present war. If America's soul becomes totally poisoned, part of the autopsy must read "Vietnam." It can never be saved so long as it destroys the deepest hopes of men the world over. So it is that those of us who are yet determined that "America will be" are led down the path of protest and dissent, working for the health of our land.

As if the weight of such a commitment to the life and health of America were not enough, another burden of responsibility was placed upon me in 1954.[1] And I cannot forget that the Nobel Peace Prize was also a commission, a commission to work harder than I had ever worked before for the brotherhood of man. This is a calling that takes me beyond national allegiances.

But even if it were not present, I would yet have to live with the meaning of my commitment to the ministry of Jesus Christ. To me, the relationship of this ministry to the making of peace

---

1. King says "1954," but most likely means 1964, the year he received the Nobel Peace Prize.

is so obvious that I sometimes marvel at those who ask me why I am speaking against the war. Could it be that they do not know that the Good News was meant for all men—for communist and capitalist, for their children and ours, for black and for white, for revolutionary and conservative? Have they forgotten that my ministry is in obedience to the one who loved his enemies so fully that he died for them? . . .

Finally, as I try to explain for you and for myself the road that leads from Montgomery to this place, I would have offered all that was most valid if I simply said that I must be true to my conviction that I share with all men the calling to be a son of the living God. Beyond the calling of race or nation or creed is this vocation of sonship and brotherhood. Because I believe that the Father is deeply concerned, especially for His suffering and helpless and outcast children, I come tonight to speak for them. This I believe to be the privilege and the burden of all of us who deem ourselves bound by allegiances and loyalties which are broader and deeper than nationalism and which go beyond our nation's self-defined goals and positions. We are called to speak for the weak, for the voiceless, for the victims of our nation, for those it calls "enemy," for no document from human hands can make these humans any less our brothers.

Speaking for the People of South Vietnam

And as I ponder the madness of Vietnam and search within myself for ways to understand and respond in compassion, my mind goes constantly to the people of that peninsula. I speak now not of the soldiers of each side, not of the ideologies of the Liberation Front, not of the junta in Saigon, but simply of the people who have been living under the curse of war for almost three continuous decades now. I think of them, too, because it is clear to me that there will be no meaningful solution there until some attempt is made to know them and hear their broken cries.

They must see Americans as strange liberators. The Vietnamese people proclaimed their own independence in 1954— in 1945 rather—after a combined French and Japanese occupation and before the communist revolution in China. They were led by Ho Chi Minh. Even though they quoted the American Declaration of Independence in their own document of freedom, we refused to recognize them. Instead, we decided to support France in its reconquest of her former colony. Our government felt then that the Vietnamese people were not ready for independence, and we again fell victim to the deadly Western arrogance that has poisoned the international atmosphere for so long. With that tragic decision we rejected a revolutionary government seeking self-determination and a government that had been established not by China—for whom the Vietnamese have no great love—but by clearly indigenous forces that included some communists. For the peasants this new government meant real land reform, one of the most important needs in their lives.

For nine years following 1945 we denied the people of Vietnam the right of independence. For nine years we vigorously supported the French in their abortive effort to recolonize Vietnam. Before the end of the war we were meeting eighty percent of the French war costs. Even before the French were defeated at Dien Bien Phu, they began to despair of their reckless action, but we did not. We encouraged them with our huge financial and military supplies to continue the war even after they had lost the will. Soon we would be paying almost the full costs of this tragic attempt at recolonization.

After the French were defeated, it looked as if independence and land reform would come again through the Geneva Agreement. But instead there came the United States, determined that Ho should not unify the temporarily divided nation, and the peasants watched again as we supported one of the most vicious modern dictators, our chosen man, Premier [Ngo Dinh] Diem. The peasants watched and cringed as Diem ruthlessly rooted out all opposition, supported their extortionist landlords, and refused even to discuss reunification with the North. The peasants watched as all of this was presided over by United States influence and then by increasing numbers of United States troops who came to help quell the insurgency that Diem's methods had aroused. When Diem was overthrown they may have been happy, but the long line of military dictators seemed to offer no real change, especially in terms of their need for land and peace.

The only change came from America as we increased our troop commitments in support of governments which were singularly corrupt, inept, and without popular support. All the while the people read our leaflets and received the regular promises of peace and democracy and land reform. Now they languish under our bombs and consider us, not their fellow Vietnamese, the real enemy. They move sadly and apathetically as we herd them off the land of their fathers into concentration camps where minimal social needs are rarely met. They know they must move on or be destroyed by our bombs.

So they go, primarily women and children and the aged. They watch as we poison their water, as we kill a million acres of their crops. They must weep as the bulldozers roar through their areas preparing to destroy the precious trees. They wander into the hospitals with at least twenty casualties from American firepower for one Vietcong-inflicted injury. So far we may have killed a million of them, mostly children. They wander into the towns and see thousands of the children, homeless, without clothes, running in packs on the streets like animals. They see the children degraded by our soldiers as they beg for food. They see the children selling their sisters to our soldiers, soliciting for their mothers.

What do the peasants think as we ally ourselves with the landlords and as we refuse to put any action into our many words concerning land reform? What do they think as we test out our latest weapons on them, just as the Germans tested out new medicine and new tortures in the concentration camps of Europe? Where are the roots of the independent Vietnam we claim to be building? Is it among these voiceless ones?

We have destroyed their two most cherished institutions: the family and the village. We have destroyed their land and their crops. We have cooperated in the crushing of the nation's only noncommunist revolutionary political force, the unified Buddhist Church. We have supported the enemies of the peasants of Saigon. We have corrupted their women and children and killed their men.

Now there is little left to build on, save bitterness. Soon the only solid physical foundations remaining will be found at our military bases and in the concrete of the concentration camps we call "fortified hamlets." The peasants may well wonder if we plan to build our new Vietnam on such grounds as these. Could we blame them for such thoughts? We must speak for them and raise the questions they cannot raise. These, too, are our brothers.

Speaking for Our Enemies

Perhaps a more difficult but no less necessary task is to speak for those who have been designated as our enemies. What of the National Liberation Front, that strangely anonymous group we call "VC" or "communists"? What must they think of the United States of America when they realize that we permitted the repression and cruelty of Diem, which helped to bring them into being as a resistance group in the South? What do they think of our condoning the violence which led to their own taking up of arms? How can they believe in our integrity when now we speak of "aggression from the North" as if there were nothing more essential to the war? How can they trust us when now we charge them with violence after the murderous reign of Diem and charge them with violence while we pour every new weapon of death into their land? Surely we must understand their feelings, even if we do not condone their actions. Surely we must see that the men we supported pressed them to their violence. Surely we must see that our own computerized plans of destruction simply dwarf their greatest acts.

How do they judge us when our officials know that their membership is less than twenty-five percent communist, and yet insist on giving them the blanket name? What must they be thinking when they know that we are aware of their control of major sections of Vietnam, and yet we appear ready to allow national elections in which this highly organized political parallel government will not have a part? They ask how we can speak of free elections when the Saigon press is censored and controlled by the military junta. And they are surely right to wonder what kind of new government we plan to help form without them, the only party in real touch with the peasants. They question our political goals and they deny the reality of a peace settlement from which they will be ex-

cluded. Their questions are frighteningly relevant. Is our nation planning to build on political myth again, and then
shore it up upon the power of a new violence?

Here is the true meaning and value of compassion and
nonviolence, when it helps us to see the enemy's point of
view, to hear his questions, to know his assessment of ourselves. For from his view we may indeed see the basic weak-
nesses of our own condition, and if we are mature, we may
learn and grow and profit from the wisdom of the brothers
who are called the opposition.

So, too, with Hanoi. In the North, where our bombs now
pummel the land, and our mines endanger the waterways, we
are met by a deep but understandable mistrust. To speak for
them is to explain this lack of confidence in Western words,
and especially their distrust of American intentions now. In
Hanoi are the men who led the nation to independence
against the Japanese and the French, the men who sought
membership in the French Commonwealth and were betrayed by the weakness of Paris and the willfulness of the
colonial armies. It was they who led a second struggle against
French domination at tremendous costs, and then were persuaded to give up the land they controlled between the thir-
teenth and seventeenth parallel as a temporary measure at
Geneva. After 1954 they watched us conspire with Diem to
prevent elections which could have surely brought Ho Chi
Minh to power over a united Vietnam, and they realized they
had been betrayed again. When we ask why they do not leap
to negotiate, these things must be remembered.

Also, it must be clear that the leaders of Hanoi considered the presence of American troops in support of the Diem
regime to have been the initial military breach of the Geneva
Agreement concerning foreign troops. They remind us that
they did not begin to send troops in large numbers and even
supplies into the South until American forces had moved into
the tens of thousands.

Hanoi remembers how our leaders refused to tell us the
truth about the earlier North Vietnamese overtures for peace,
how the president claimed that none existed when they had
clearly been made. Ho Chi Minh has watched as America has
spoken of peace and built up its forces, and now he has

surely heard the increasing international rumors of American plans for an invasion of the North. He knows the bombing and shelling and mining we are doing are part of traditional pre-invasion strategy. Perhaps only his sense of humor and of irony can save him when he hears the most powerful nation of the world speaking of aggression as it drops thousands of bombs on a poor, weak nation more than eight hundred, or rather, eight thousand miles away from its shores.

At this point I should make it clear that while I have tried in these last few minutes to give a voice to the voiceless in Vietnam and to understand the arguments of those who are called "enemy," I am as deeply concerned about our own troops there as anything else. For it occurs to me that what we are submitting them to in Vietnam is not simply the brutalizing process that goes on in any war where armies face each other and seek to destroy. We are adding cynicism to the process of death, for they must know after a short period there that none of the things we claim to be fighting for are really involved. Before long they must know that their government has sent them into a struggle among Vietnamese, and the more sophisticated surely realize that we are on the side of the wealthy, and the secure, while we create a hell for the poor.

The Madness Must Cease

Somehow this madness must cease. We must stop now. I speak as a child of God and brother to the suffering poor of Vietnam. I speak for those whose land is being laid waste, whose homes are being destroyed, whose culture is being subverted. I speak for the poor of America who are paying the double price of smashed hopes at home, and dealt death and corruption in Vietnam. I speak as a citizen of the world, for the world as it stands aghast at the path we have taken. I speak as one who loves America, to the leaders of our own nation: The great initiative in this war is ours; the initiative to stop it must be ours. . . .

If we continue, there will be no doubt in my mind and in the mind of the world that we have no honorable intentions in Vietnam. If we do not stop our war against the people of

Vietnam immediately, the world will be left with no other alternative than to see this as some horrible, clumsy, and deadly game we have decided to play. The world now demands a maturity of America that we may not be able to achieve. It demands that we admit that we have been wrong from the beginning of our adventure in Vietnam, that we have been detrimental to the life of the Vietnamese people. The situation is one in which we must be ready to turn sharply from our present ways. In order to atone for our sins and errors in Vietnam, we should take the initiative in bringing a halt to this tragic war. . . .

Vietnam as a Symptom

Now there is something seductively tempting about stopping there and sending us all off on what in some circles has become a popular crusade against the war in Vietnam. I say we must enter that struggle, but I wish to go on now to say something even more disturbing.

The war in Vietnam is but a symptom of a far deeper malady within the American spirit, and if we ignore this sobering reality, we will find ourselves organizing "clergy and laymen concerned" committees for the next generation. They will be concerned about Guatemala and Peru. They will be concerned about Thailand and Cambodia. They will be concerned about Mozambique and South Africa. We will be marching for these and a dozen other names and attending rallies without end unless there is a significant and profound change in American life and policy. So such thoughts take us beyond Vietnam, but not beyond our calling as sons of the living God.

In 1957 a sensitive American official overseas said that it seemed to him that our nation was on the wrong side of a world revolution. During the past ten years we have seen emerge a pattern of suppression which has now justified the presence of U.S. military advisors in Venezuela. This need to maintain social stability for our investments accounts for the counterrevolutionary action of American forces in Guatemala. It tells why American helicopters are being used against guerrillas in Cambodia and why American napalm and Green

Beret forces have already been active against rebels in Peru.

It is with such activity in mind that the words of the late [President] John F. Kennedy come back to haunt us. Five years ago he said, "Those who make peaceful revolution impossible will make violent revolution inevitable." Increasingly, by choice or by accident, this is the role our nation has taken, the role of those who make peaceful revolution impossible by refusing to give up the privileges and the pleasures that come from the immense profits of overseas investments. I am convinced that if we are to get on the right side of the world revolution, we as a nation must undergo a radical revolution of values. We must rapidly begin the shift from a thing-oriented society to a person-oriented society. When machines and computers, profit motives and property rights, are considered more important than people, the giant triplets of racism, extreme materialism, and militarism are incapable of being conquered.

A True Revolution of Values

A true revolution of values will soon cause us to question the fairness and justice of many of our past and present policies. . . . True compassion is more than flinging a coin to a beggar. It comes to see that an edifice which produces beggars needs restructuring.

A true revolution of values will soon look uneasily on the glaring contrast of poverty and wealth. With righteous indignation, it will look across the seas and see individual capitalists of the West investing huge sums of money in Asia, Africa, and South America, only to take the profits out with no concern for the social betterment of the countries, and say, "This is not just." It will look at our alliance with the landed gentry of South America and say, "This is not just." The Western arrogance of feeling that it has everything to teach others and nothing to learn from them is not just.

A true revolution of values will lay hand on the world order and say of war, "This way of settling differences is not just." This business of burning human beings with napalm, of filling our nation's homes with orphans and widows, of injecting poisonous drugs of hate into the veins of peoples normally humane, of sending men home from dark and bloody battlefields physically handicapped and psychologically deranged, cannot be reconciled with wisdom, justice, and love. A nation that continues year after year to spend more money on military defense than on programs of social uplift is approaching spiritual death. . . .

This kind of positive revolution of values is our best defense against communism. War is not the answer. Communism will never be defeated by the use of atomic bombs or nuclear weapons. Let us not join those who shout war and, through their misguided passions, urge the United States to relinquish its participation in the United Nations. These are days which demand wise restraint and calm reasonableness. We must not engage in a negative anticommunism, but rather in a positive thrust for democracy, realizing that our greatest defense against communism is to take offensive action in behalf of justice. We must with positive action seek to remove those conditions of poverty, insecurity, and injustice, which are the fertile soil in which the seed of communism grows and develops.

These are revolutionary times. All over the globe men are revolting against old systems of exploitation and oppression, and out of the wounds of a frail world, new systems of justice and equality are being born. The shirtless and barefoot people of the land are rising up as never before. The people who sat in darkness have seen a great light. We in the West must support these revolutions.

It is a sad fact that because of comfort, complacency, a morbid fear of communism, and our proneness to adjust to injustice, the Western nations that initiated so much of the revolutionary spirit of the modern world have now become the arch antirevolutionaries. This has driven many to feel that only Marxism has a revolutionary spirit. Therefore, communism is a judgment against our failure to make democracy real and follow through on the revolutions that we initiated. Our only hope today lies in our ability to recapture the revolutionary spirit and go out into a sometimes hostile world declaring eternal hostility to poverty, racism, and militarism. With this powerful commitment we shall boldly challenge the status quo and unjust mores, and thereby speed the day when "every valley shall be exalted, and every mountain and hill shall be made low; the crooked shall be made straight, and the rough places plain."

A genuine revolution of values means in the final analysis that our loyalties must become ecumenical rather than sectional. Every nation must now develop an overriding loyalty to mankind as a whole in order to preserve the best in their individual societies. . . .

Now let us begin. Now let us rededicate ourselves to the long and bitter, but beautiful, struggle for a new world. This is the calling of the sons of God, and our brothers wait eagerly for our response. Shall we say the odds are too great? Shall we tell them the struggle is too hard? Will our message be that the forces of American life militate against their arrival as full men, and we send our deepest regrets? Or will there be another message—of longing, of hope, of solidarity with their yearnings, of commitment to their cause, whatever the cost? The choice is ours, and though we might prefer it otherwise, we must choose in this crucial moment of human history. . . .

And if we will only make the right choice, we will be able to transform this pending cosmic elegy into a creative psalm of peace. If we will make the right choice, we will be able to transform the jangling discords of our world into a beautiful symphony of brotherhood. If we will but make the right choice, we will be able to speed up the day, all over America and all over the world, when justice will roll down like waters, and righteousness like a mighty stream.

U.S. Imperial Foreign Policy Is Creating Two Wars: The War Abroad and the War at Home

J. William Fulbright

As a United States senator from 1945 through 1974, J. William Fulbright helped guide the United States through most of the thirty years of America's longest war, the Vietnam War. After helping pass the Gulf of Tonkin Resolution giving President Lyndon B. Johnson war-making powers in Southeast Asia, Senator Fulbright became disturbed to learn that officials in the Johnson administration had misled him about the Gulf of Tonkin events. As Johnson escalated American involvement in the war during 1965, Fulbright became convinced that the Gulf of Tonkin Resolution had been a mistake and that U.S. foreign policy was fundamentally flawed. As chairman of the Senate Foreign Relations Committee, he began hearings on the conduct of the Vietnam War in January 1966 and, subsequently, he began a public campaign to rescind the Gulf of Tonkin Resolution and to extract the United States from Vietnam.

In the following speech, delivered on August 8, 1967, at an American Bar Association luncheon in Honolulu, Hawaii, Senator Fulbright examines the conflict in American values between the imperial role of the United States as the world's policeman and the demands of freedom

Excerpted from J. William Fulbright's speech before the American Bar Association, August 8, 1967.

and social justice at home. He questions whether President Lyndon Johnson's administration has the moral capacity to manage both a war and the Great Society (Johnson's ambitious program for solving American social problems), and suggests that the United States is fighting both a war in Vietnam and a war at home and that both wars are contributing to a deterioration of American society. The wars are related, he argues, because the Vietnam War diverts resources from social problems in the United States and legitimates the use of violence to solve problems in Vietnam and in the United States. While imperial arrogance and lack of moral leadership sickens American society, Fulbright finds optimism in the activism of youthful Americans who, as a measure of their integrity and idealism, protest inhumanity and injustice in Vietnam and in the United States.

Although other Vietnam War critics had indicted U.S. foreign policy for being imperialist, Fulbright's powerful and eloquent oratory and his reputation as one of the wisest and most distinguished men in government contributed substantial credibility to the criticism. Fulbright would finally see the Gulf of Tonkin Resolution rescinded in November 1973, when Congress passed the War Powers Act over the veto of President Richard Nixon.

Standing in the smoke and rubble of Detroit, a Negro veteran said: "I just got back from Vietnam a few months ago, but you know, I think the war is here."

There are in fact two wars going on. One is the war of power politics which our soldiers are fighting in the jungles of southeast Asia. The other is a war for America's soul which is being fought in the streets of Newark and Detroit and in the halls of Congress, in churches and protest meetings and on college campuses, and in the hearts and minds of silent Americans from Maine to Hawaii. I believe that the two wars have something to do with each other, not in the direct, tangibly causal way that bureaucrats require as proof of a connection between two things, but in a subtler, moral and qualitative way that is no less real for being intangible. Each of these wars might well be going on in the absence of the other, but neither, I suspect, standing alone, would seem so hopeless and demoralizing.

The connection between Vietnam and Detroit is in their conflicting and incompatible demands upon traditional American values. The one demands that they be set aside, the other that they be fulfilled. The one demands the acceptance by America of an imperial role in the world, or of what our policy makers like to call the "responsibilities of power," or of what I have called the "arrogance of power." The other demands freedom and social justice at home, an end to poverty, the fulfillment of our flawed democracy, and an effort to create a role for ourselves in the world which is compatible with our traditional values. The question, it should be emphasized, is not whether it is *possible* to engage in traditional power politics abroad and at the same time to perfect democracy at home, but whether it is possible for *us Americans,* with our particular history and national character, to combine morally incompatible roles.

Administration officials tell us that we can indeed afford both Vietnam and the Great Society, and they produce impressive statistics of the gross national product to prove it. The statistics show financial capacity but they do not show moral and psychological capacity. They do not show how a President preoccupied with bombing missions over North and South Vietnam can provide strong and consistent leadership for the renewal of our cities. They do not show how a Congress burdened with war costs and war measures, with emergency briefings and an endless series of dramatic appeals, with anxious constituents and a mounting anxiety of their own, can tend to the workaday business of studying social problems and legislating programs to meet them. Nor do the statistics tell how an anxious and puzzled people, bombarded by press and television with the bad news of American deaths in Vietnam, the "good news" of enemy deaths— and with vividly horrifying pictures to illustrate them—can be expected to support neighborhood anti-poverty projects and national programs for urban renewal, employment and education. Anxiety about war does not breed compassion for one's neighbors; nor do constant reminders of the cheapness of life abroad strengthen our faith in its sanctity at home. In these ways the war in Vietnam is poisoning and brutalizing our domestic life. Psychological incompatibility has proven to be more controlling than financial feasibility; and the Great Society has become a sick society.

Imperial Destiny and the American Dream

When he visited America a hundred years ago, Thomas Huxley wrote: "I cannot say that I am in the slightest degree impressed by your bigness, or your material resources, as such. Size is not grandeur, and territory does not make a nation. The great issue, about which hangs the terror of overhanging fate, is what are you going to do with all these things?"

The question is still with us and we seem to have come to a time of historical crisis when its answer can no longer be deferred. Before the Second World War our world role was a *potential* role; we were important in the world for what we *could* do with our power, for the leadership we *might* provide, for the example we *might* set. Now the choices are almost gone: we are *almost* the world's self-appointed policeman; we are *almost* the world defender of the *status quo*. We are well on our way to becoming a traditional great power—an imperial nation if you will—engaged in the exercise of power for its own sake, exercising it to the limit of our capacity and beyond, filling every vacuum and extending the American "presence" to the farthest reaches of the earth. And, as with the great empires of the past, as the power grows, it is becoming an end in itself, separated except by ritual incantation from its initial motives, governed, it would seem, by its own mystique, power without philosophy or purpose.

That describes what we have *almost* become, but we have not become a traditional empire yet. The old values remain—the populism and the optimism, the individualism and the rough-hewn equality, the friendliness and the good humor, the inventiveness and the zest for life, the caring about people and the sympathy for the underdog, and the idea, which goes back to the American Revolution, that maybe—just maybe—we can set an example of democracy and human dignity for the world.

That is something which none of the great empires of the past has ever done—or tried to do—or wanted to do—but we were bold enough—or presumptuous enough—to think that we might be able to do it. And there are a great many Americans who still think we can do it—or at least they want to try.

That, I believe, is what all the hue and cry is about—the dissent in the Senate and the protest marches in the cities, the letters to the President from student leaders and former Peace Corps volunteers, the lonely searching of conscience by a student facing the draft and the letter to a Senator from a soldier in the field who can no longer accept the official explanations of why he has been sent to fight in the jungles of Vietnam. All believe that their country was cut out for something more ennobling than an imperial destiny. Our youth are showing that they still believe in the American dream, and their protests attest to its continuing vitality. . . .

The students and churchmen and professors who are protesting the Vietnam war do not accept the notion that foreign policy is a matter of expedients to which values are irrelevant. They reject this notion because they understand, as some of our policy makers do not understand, that it is ultimately self-defeating to "fight fire with fire," that you cannot defend your values in a manner that does violence to those values without destroying the very thing you are trying to defend. They understand, as our policy makers do not, that when American soldiers are sent, in the name of freedom, to sustain corrupt dictators in a civil war, that when the CIA subverts student organizations to engage in propaganda activities abroad, or when the Export-Import Bank is used by the Pentagon to finance secret arms sales abroad, damage—perhaps irreparable damage—is being done to the very values that are meant to be defended. The critics understand, as our policy makers do not, that, through the undemocratic expedients we have adopted for the defense of American democracy, we are weakening it to a degree that is beyond the resources of our bitterest enemies. . . .

The critics of our current course also challenge the contention that the traditional methods of foreign policy are safe and prudent and realistic. They are understandably skeptical of their wise and experienced elders who, in the name of prudence, caution against any departure from the tried and true methods that have led in this century to Sarajevo, Munich and Dien Bien Phu. They think that the methods of the past have been tried and found wanting, and two world wars attest powerfully to their belief. Most of all, they think that, in this first era of human history in which man has acquired weapons which threaten his entire species with destruction, safety and prudence and realism require us to change the rules of a dangerous and discredited game, to try as we have never tried before to civilize and humanize international relations, not only for the sake of civilization and humanity but for the sake of survival.

Even the most ardent advocates of an imperial role for the United States would probably agree that the proper objective of our foreign policy is the fostering of a world environment in which we can, with reasonable security, devote our main energies to the realization of the values of our own society. This does not require the adoption or imposition of these values on anybody, but it does require us so to conduct ourselves that our society does not seem hateful and repugnant to others.

At present much of the world is repelled by America and what America seems to stand for in the world. Both in our foreign affairs and in our domestic life we convey an image of violence; I do not care very much about images as distinguished from the things they reflect, but this image is rooted in reality. Abroad we are engaged in a savage and unsuccessful war against poor people in a small and backward nation. At home—largely because of the neglect resulting from twenty-five years of preoccupation with foreign involvements—our cities are exploding in violent protest against generations of social injustice. America, which only a few years ago seemed to the world to be a model of democracy and social justice, has become a symbol of violence and undisciplined power.

" . . . it is excellent," wrote Shakespeare, "to have a giant's strength; but it is tyrannous to use it like a giant."[1] By using

1. *Measure for Measure*, Act II, Scene 2, Line 107.

our power like a giant we are fostering a world environment which is, to put it mildly, uncongenial to our society. By our undisciplined use of physical power we have divested ourselves of a greater power: the power of example. How, for example, can we commend peaceful compromise to the Arabs and the Israelis when we are unwilling to suspend our relentless bombing of North Vietnam? How can we commend democratic social reform to Latin America when Newark, Detroit, and Milwaukee are providing explosive evidence of our own inadequate efforts at democratic social reform? How can we commend the free enterprise system to Asians and Africans when in our own country it has produced vast, chaotic, noisy, dangerous and dirty urban complexes while poisoning the very air and land and water? There may come a time when Americans will again be able to commend their country as an example to the world and, more in hope than confidence, I retain my faith that there will; but to do so right at this moment would take more gall than I have.

Far from building a safe world environment for American values, our war in Vietnam and the domestic deterioration which it has aggravated are creating a most uncongenial world atmosphere for American ideas and values. The world has no need, in this age of nationalism and nuclear weapons, for a new imperial power, but there is a great need of moral leadership—by which I mean the leadership of decent example. That role could be ours but we have vacated the field, and all that has kept the Russians from filling it is their own lack of imagination.

At the same time, as we have noted, and of even greater fundamental importance, our purposeless and undisciplined use of power is causing a profound controversy in our own society. This in a way is something to be proud of. We have sickened but not succumbed and just as a healthy body fights disease, we are fighting the alien concept which is being thrust upon us, not by history but by our policy makers in the Department of State and the Pentagon. We are proving the strength of the American dream by resisting the dream of an imperial destiny. We are demonstrating the validity of our traditional values by the difficulty we are having in betraying them.

The principal defenders of these values are our remarkable younger generation, something of whose spirit is expressed in a letter which I received from an American soldier in Vietnam. Speaking of the phony propaganda on both sides, and then of the savagery of the war, or the people he describes as the "real casualties"—"the farmers and their families in the Delta mangled by air strikes, and the villagers here killed and burned out by our friendly Korean mercenaries"—this young soldier then asks ". . . whatever has become of our dream? Where is that America that opposed tyrannies at every turn, without inquiring first whether some particular forms of tyranny might be of use to us? Of the three rights which men have, the first, as I recall, was the right to life. How then have we come to be killing so many in such a dubious cause?"

The Sick Society

While the death toll mounts in Vietnam, it is mounting too in the war at home. During a single week of July 1967, 164 Americans were killed and 1,442 wounded in Vietnam, while 65 Americans were killed and 2,100 were wounded in city riots in the United States. We are truly fighting a two-front war and doing badly in both. Each war feeds on the other and, although the President assures us that we have the resources to win both wars, in fact we are not winning either.

Together the two wars have set in motion a process of deterioration in American society and there is no question that each of the two crises is heightened by the impact of the other. Not only does the Vietnam war divert human and material resources from our festering cities; not only does it foster the conviction on the part of slum Negroes that their country is indifferent to their plight. In addition the war feeds the idea of violence as a way of solving problems. If, as Mr. [U.S. Secretary of State Dean] Rusk tells us, only the rain of bombs can bring Ho Chi Minh to reason, why should not the same principle apply at home? Why should not riots and snipers' bullets bring the white man to an awareness of the Negro's plight when peaceful programs for housing and jobs and training have been more rhetoric than reality? Ugly and shocking thoughts are in the American air and they were forged in the Vietnam crucible. Black power extremists talk of "wars of liberation" in the urban ghettoes of America. A cartoon in a London newspaper showed two Negro soldiers in battle in Vietnam with one saying to the other: "This is going to be great training for civilian life."

The effect of domestic violence on the chances for peace in Vietnam may turn out to be no less damaging than the impact of the war on events at home. With their limited knowledge of the United States, the Vietcong and the North Vietnamese may regard the urban riots as a harbinger of impending breakdown and eventual American withdrawal from Vietnam, warranting stepped up warfare and an uncompromising position on negotiations. It is possible that the several opportunities to negotiate which our government has let pass, most recently last winter, could not now be retrieved. Some eighteen months ago General Maxwell Taylor said in testimony before the Senate Foreign Relations Committee that the war was being prolonged by domestic dissent. That dissent was based in part on apprehension as to the effects of the war on our domestic life. Now the war is being prolonged by the domestic deterioration which has in fact occurred and it is doubtful that all of the dissenters in America, even if they wanted to, as they certainly do not, could give the enemy a fraction of the aid and comfort that has been given him by Newark, Detroit and Milwaukee.

An unnecessary and immoral war deserves in its own right to be liquidated; when its effect in addition is the aggravation of grave problems and the corrosion of values in our own society, its liquidation under terms of reasonable and honorable compromise is doubly imperative. Our country is being weakened by a grotesque inversion of priorities, the effects of which are becoming clear to more and more Americans—in the Congress, in the press and in the country at large. . . .

Priorities are reflected in the things we spend money on. Far from being a dry accounting of bookkeepers, a nation's budget is full of moral implications; it tells what a society cares about and what it does not care about; it tells what its values are.

Here are a few statistics on America's values: Since 1946 we have spent over $1,578 billion through our regular national budget. Of this amount over $904 billion, or 57.29 percent of the total, have gone for military power. By contrast, less than $96 billion, or 6.08 percent, were spent on "social functions" including education, health, labor and welfare programs, housing and community development. The Administration's budget for fiscal year 1968 calls for almost $76 billion to be spent on the military and only $15 billion for "social functions."

I would not say that we have shown ourselves to value weapons five or ten times as much as we value domestic social needs, as the figures suggest; certainly much of our military spending has been necessitated by genuine requirements of national security. I think, however, that we have embraced the necessity with excessive enthusiasm, that the Congress has been all too willing to provide unlimited sums for the military and not really very reluctant at all to offset these costs to a very small degree by cutting away funds for the poverty program and urban renewal, for rent supplements for the poor and even for a program to help protect slum children from being bitten by rats. . . .

The Regenerative Power of Youth

While the country sickens for lack of moral leadership, a most remarkable younger generation has taken up the standard of American idealism. Unlike so many of their elders, they have perceived the fraud and sham in American life and are unequivocally rejecting it. Some, the hippies, have simply withdrawn, and while we may regret the loss of their energies and their sense of decency, we can hardly gainsay their evaluation of the state of society. Others of our youth are sardonic and skeptical, not, I think, because they do not want ideals but because they want the genuine article and will not tolerate fraud. Others—students who wrestle with their consciences about the draft, soldiers who wrestle with their consciences about the war, Peace Corps volunteers who strive to light the spark of human dignity among the poor of India or Brazil, and VISTA [Volunteers In Service To America] volunteers who try to do the same for our own poor in Harlem or Appalachia—are striving to keep alive the traditional values of American democracy.

They are not really radical, these young idealists, no more radical, that is, than [former President Thomas] Jefferson's idea of freedom, [former President Abraham] Lincoln's idea of equality, or [former President Woodrow] Wilson's idea of a peaceful community of nations. Some of them, it is true, are taking what many regard as radical action, but they are doing it in defense of traditional values and in protest against the radical departure from those values embodied in the idea of an imperial destiny for America.

The focus of their protest is the war in Vietnam and the measure of their integrity is the fortitude with which they refused to be deceived about it. By striking contrast with the young Germans who accepted the Nazi evil because the values of their society had disintegrated and they had no normal frame of reference, these young Americans are demonstrating the vitality of American values. They are demonstrating that, while their country is capable of acting falsely to itself, it cannot do so without internal disruption, without calling forth the regenerative counterforce of protest from Americans who are willing to act in defense of the principles they were brought up to believe in. . . .

Now the possession of their souls is being challenged by the false and dangerous dream of an imperial destiny. It may be that the challenge will succeed, that America will succumb to becoming a traditional empire and will reign for a time over what must surely be a moral if not a physical wasteland, and then, like the great empires of the past, will decline or fall. Or it may be that the effort to create so grotesque an anachronism will go up in flames of nuclear holocaust. But if I had to bet my money on what is going to happen, I would bet on this younger generation—this generation who reject the inhumanity of war in a poor and distant land, who reject the poverty and sham in their own country, this generation who are telling their elders what their elders ought to have known, that the price of empire is America's soul and that price is too high.

The United States Cannot Win the Vietnam War

Robert F. Kennedy

On January 30, 1968, during Tet, the Vietnamese New Year, Vietminh and Vietcong forces collectively began a massive military campaign against South Vietnamese strongholds. In bloody fighting that lasted nearly a month, U.S. and South Vietnamese forces eventually repelled the attack. Although Communist forces lost one-fifth of their soldiers and never fully controlled any territory, the Tet Offensive discredited optimistic reports by American leaders and demoralized Americans with the suggestion that the Vietnam War was far from over.

As attorney general for his brother, President John F. Kennedy, Robert F. Kennedy participated in the early escalation of American presence in Vietnam. As U.S. senator in the years following his brother's assassination, he began to doubt the wisdom of American intervention in Southeast Asia. Speaking on February 8, 1968, at the height of the North Vietnamese Tet Offensive, Senator Kennedy, who had heard General William Westmoreland's address to Congress on April 28, 1967, criticizes the overly optimistic reports of U.S. military leaders about the progress of the war in the light of the Tet Offensive. He argues, as his brother John Kennedy had argued in 1954, that the South Vietnamese people do not support the government of South Vietnam and without their support U.S. efforts are futile.

Kennedy became a presidential candidate on March

Excerpted from Robert F. Kennedy's speech before the United States Senate, February 8, 1968.

16, 1968, running on an antiwar platform and winning several primary elections. Tragically, his assassination on June 5, 1968, less than four months after this address, prematurely ended his campaign for the presidency and his quest for a peaceful resolution in Southeast Asia.

Our enemy, savagely striking at will across all of South Vietnam, has finally shattered the mask of official illusion with which we have concealed our true circumstances, even from ourselves. But a short time ago we were serene in our reports and predictions of progress.

The Vietcong will probably withdraw from the cities, as they were forced to withdraw from the American Embassy. Thousands of them will be dead.

But they will, nevertheless, have demonstrated that no part or person of South Vietnam is secure from their attacks: neither district capitals nor American bases, neither the peasant in his rice paddy nor the commanding general of our own great forces.

No one can predict the exact shape or outcome of the battles now in progress, in Saigon or at Khesanh. Let us pray that we will succeed at the lowest possible cost to our young men.

But whatever their outcome, the events of the last two weeks have taught us something. For the sake of those young Americans who are fighting today, if for no other reason, the time has come to take a new look at the war in Vietnam; not by cursing the past but by using it to illuminate the future.

Facts and Illusions

And the first and necessary step is to face the facts. It is to seek out the austere and painful reality of Vietnam, freed from wishful thinking, false hopes and sentimental dreams. It is to rid ourselves of the "good company," of those illusions which have lured us into the deepening swamp of Vietnam.

We must, first of all, rid ourselves of the illusion that the events of the past two weeks represent some sort of victory. That is not so.

It is said the Vietcong will not be able to hold the cities. This is probably true. But they have demonstrated despite all our reports of progress, of government strength and enemy weakness, that half a million American soldiers with 700,000 Vietnamese allies, with total command of the air, total command of the sea, backed by huge resources and the most modern weapons, are unable to secure even a single city from the attacks of an enemy whose total strength is about 250,000. . . .

For years we have been told that the measure of our success and progress in Vietnam was increasing security and control for the population. Now we have seen that none of the population is secure and no area is under sure control.

Four years ago when we only had about 30,000 troops in Vietnam, the Vietcong were unable to mount the assaults on cities they have now conducted against our enormous forces. At one time a suggestion that we protect enclaves was derided. Now there are no protected enclaves.

The Will of the People

This has not happened because our men are not brave or effective, because they are. It is because we have misconceived the nature of the war: It is because we have sought to resolve by military might a conflict whose issue depends upon the will and conviction of the South Vietnamese people. It is like sending a lion to halt an epidemic of jungle rot.

This misconception rests on a second illusion—the illusion that we can win a war which the South Vietnamese cannot win for themselves.

You cannot expect people to risk their lives and endure hardship unless they have a stake in their own society. They must have a clear sense of identification with their own government, a belief they are participating in a cause worth fighting for.

People will not fight to line the pockets of generals or swell the bank accounts of the wealthy. They are far more likely to close their eyes and shut their doors in the face of their government—even as they did last week.

More than any election, more than any proud boast, that single fact reveals the truth. We have an ally in name only. We

support a government without supporters. Without the efforts of American arms that government would not last a day.

The third illusion is that the unswerving pursuit of military victory, whatever its cost, is in the interest of either ourselves or the people of Vietnam.

For the people of Vietnam, the last three years have
meant little but horror. Their tiny land has been devastated
by a weight of bombs and shells greater than Nazi Germany
knew in the Second World War.

We have dropped 12 tons of bombs for every square mile
in North and South Vietnam. Whole provinces have been
substantially destroyed. More than two million South Vietnamese are now homeless refugees.

Imagine the impact in our own country if an equivalent
number—over 25 million Americans—were wandering homeless or interned in refugee camps, and millions more refugees
were being created as New York and Chicago, Washington
and Boston, were being destroyed by a war raging in their
streets.

Whatever the outcome of these battles, it is the people we
seek to defend who are the greatest losers.

Nor does it serve the interests of America to fight this
war as if moral standards could be subordinated to immediate necessities. Last week, a Vietcong suspect was turned
over to the chief of the Vietnamese Security Services, who executed him on the spot—a flat violation of the Geneva Convention on the Rules of War.

The photograph of the execution was on front pages all
around the world—leading our best and oldest friends to
ask, more in sorrow than in anger, what has happened to
America?

The National Interest

The fourth illusion is that the American national interest is
identical with—or should be subordinated to—the selfish interest of an incompetent military regime.

We are told, of course, that the battle for South Vietnam
is in reality a struggle for 250 million Asians—the beginning
of a Great Society for all of Asia. But this is pretension.

We can and should offer reasonable assistance to Asia; but we cannot build a Great Society there if we cannot build one in our own country. We cannot speak extravagantly of a struggle for 250 million Asians, when a struggle for 15 million in one Asian country so strains our forces, that another Asian country, a fourth-rate power which we have already once defeated in battle, dares to seize an American ship and hold and humiliate her crew. [On January 23, 1968, the USS *Pueblo*, an American naval intelligence ship, and its crew were seized by North Korea while patrolling Korea's coastal waters.]

The fifth illusion is that this war can be settled in our own way and in our own time on our own terms. Such a settlement is the privilege of the triumphant: of those who crush their enemies in battle or wear away their will to fight.

We have not done this, nor is there any prospect we will achieve such a victory.

Unable to defeat our enemy or break his will—at least without a huge, long and ever more costly effort—we must actively seek a peaceful settlement. We can no longer harden our terms every time Hanoi indicates it may be prepared to negotiate; and we must be willing to foresee a settlement which will give the Vietcong a chance to participate in the political life of the country.

Basic Truths

These are some of the illusions which may be discarded if the events of last week are to prove not simply a tragedy, but a lesson: a lesson which carries with it some basic truths.

First, that a total military victory is not within sight or around the corner; that, in fact, it is probably beyond our grasp; and that the effort to win such a victory will only result in the further slaughter of thousands of innocent and helpless people—a slaughter which will forever rest on our national conscience.

Second, that the pursuit of such a victory is not necessary to our national interest, and is even damaging that interest.

Third, that the progress we have claimed toward increasing our control over the country and the security of the population is largely illusory.

Fourth, that the central battle in this war cannot be measured by body counts or bomb damage, but by the extent to which the people of South Vietnam act on a sense of common purpose and hope with those that govern them.

Fifth, that the current regime in Saigon is unwilling or incapable of being an effective ally in the war against the Communists.

Sixth, that a political compromise is not just the best path to peace, but the only path, and we must show as much willingness to risk some of our prestige for peace as to risk the lives of young men in war.

Seventh, that the escalation policy in Vietnam, far from strengthening and consolidating international resistance to aggression, is injuring our country through the world, reducing the faith of other peoples in our wisdom and purpose and weakening the world's resolve to stand together for freedom and peace.

Eighth, that the best way to save our most precious stake in Vietnam—the lives of our soldiers—is to stop the enlargement of the war, and that the best way to end casualties is to end the war.

Ninth, that our nation must be told the truth about this war, in all its terrible reality, both because it is right—and because only in this way can any Administration rally the public confidence and unity for the shadowed days which lie ahead.

No war has ever demanded more bravery from our people and our Government—not just bravery under fire or the bravery to make sacrifices—but the bravery to discard the comfort of illusion—to do away with false hopes and alluring promises.

Reality is grim and painful. But it is only a remote echo of the anguish toward which a policy founded on illusion is surely taking us.

This is a great nation and a strong people. Any who seek to comfort rather than speak plainly, reassure rather than instruct, promise satisfaction rather than reveal frustration—they deny that greatness and drain that strength. For today as it was in the beginning, it is the truth that makes us free.

CHAPTER
FIVE

American
Withdrawal

De-Escalation and Renunciation in Search of Peace in Vietnam

Lyndon B. Johnson

After assuming the presidency upon John F. Kennedy's assassination in November 1963, Lyndon B. Johnson ran for election and was elected in 1964 by the widest popular margin in American presidential history. At that time he had already served in the government for more than twenty years. Johnson's upbringing in poor, rural Texas inspired his Great Society program, legislative initiatives that included aid to education and health, children's vaccinations, Medicare, Medicaid, urban renewal, beautification, conservation, development of depressed regions, housing and community development, a war against poverty, control and prevention of crime, civil rights, removing obstacles to the right to vote, and space exploration. However, Johnson's plans to improve life for Americans at home were greatly limited by the Vietnam War, which forced him to shift his focus from domestic issues to foreign policy issues. Moreover, as the war continued, an increasing number of Americans expressed their dissatisfaction with the war, and some of his supporters and advisers began to desert him. After U.S. and South Vietnamese forces repelled the massive Communist Tet Offensive in nearly a month of fighting early in 1968, Johnson asked Secretary of Defense Clark Clifford to conduct a thorough review of U.S. policy in Vietnam.

Excerpted from Lyndon B. Johnson's televised address to the American people, March 31, 1968.

Late in March, Clifford and Johnson's advisers counseled against more troop increases in Vietnam.

In the following speech, a live television address to the nation on March 31, 1968, President Johnson declares his intention to de-escalate the Vietnam War by suspending the bombing of North Vietnam in an effort to invite peace negotiations with the North Vietnamese. He reaffirms the vision he expressed in his Johns Hopkins address three years earlier for economic development in South Vietnam and quotes John F. Kennedy's inaugural address in defense of his conduct of the war, but he announces that he is withdrawing as a candidate for reelection so that he can seek peace in Southeast Asia unimpeded by politics.

The North Vietnamese responded to Johnson's de-escalation by agreeing to peace talks in Paris, France, in May 1968. In October 1968, negotiators reached an agreement and Johnson halted the bombing of North Vietnam, which he had begun in February 1965. On November 2, 1968, however, South Vietnamese President Nguyen Van Thieu, assured by Richard Nixon that he would get a better deal later, refused to support the Paris agreement. Nixon won the U.S. presidential election a few days later.

T onight I want to speak to you of peace in Vietnam and Southeast Asia.

No other question so preoccupies our people. No other dream so absorbs the 250 million human beings who live in that part of the world. No other goal motivates American policy in Southeast Asia.

For years, representatives of our Government and others have traveled the world—seeking to find a basis for peace talks.

Since last September, they have carried the offer that I made public at San Antonio.

That offer was this:

That the United States would stop its bombardment of

North Vietnam when that would lead promptly to productive discussions—and that we would assume that North Vietnam would not take military advantage of our restraint.

Hanoi denounced this offer, both privately and publicly. Even while the search for peace was going on, North Vietnam rushed their preparations for a savage assault on the people, the government, and the allies of South Vietnam.

Their attack—during the Tet holidays—failed to achieve its principal objectives. It did not collapse the elected government of South Vietnam or shatter its army—as the Communists had hoped.

It did not produce a "general uprising" among the people of the cities as they had predicted.

The Communists were unable to maintain control of any of the more than 30 cities that they attacked. And they took very heavy casualties.

But they did compel the South Vietnamese and their allies to move certain forces from the countryside into the cities.

They caused widespread disruption and suffering. Their attacks, and the battles that followed, made refugees of half a million human beings.

The Communists may renew their attack any day.

They are, it appears, trying to make 1968 the year of decision in South Vietnam—the year that brings, if not final victory or defeat, at least a turning point in the struggle.

This much is clear:

If they do mount another round of heavy attacks, they will not succeed in destroying the fighting power of South Vietnam and its allies.

But tragically, this is also clear: Many men—on both sides of the struggle—will be lost. A nation that has already suffered 20 years of warfare will suffer once again.

Armies on both sides will take new casualties. And the war will go on.

There is no need for this to be so.

There is no need to delay the talks that could bring an end to this long and this bloody war.

Tonight, I renew the offer I made last August to stop the bombardment of North Vietnam. We ask that talks begin promptly, that they be serious talks on the substance of peace. We assume that during those talks Hanoi will not take advantage of our restraint.

We are prepared to move immediately toward peace through negotiations.

De-Escalation of the War

So, tonight, in the hope that this action will lead to early talks, I am taking the first step to de-escalate the conflict. We are reducing—substantially reducing the present level of hostilities.

And we are doing so unilaterally, and at once.

Tonight, I have ordered our aircraft and our naval vessels to make no attacks on North Vietnam, except in the area north of the demilitarized zone where the continuing enemy buildup directly threatens allied forward positions and where the movements of their troops and supplies are clearly related to that threat.

The area in which we are stopping our attacks includes almost 90 percent of North Vietnam's population, and most of its territory. Thus there will be no attacks around the principal populated areas, or in the food-producing areas of North Vietnam.

Even this very limited bombing of the North could come to an early end—if our restraint is matched by restraint in Hanoi. But I cannot in good conscience stop all bombing so long as to do so would immediately and directly endanger the lives of our men and our allies. Whether a complete bombing halt becomes possible in the future will be determined by events.

Our purpose in this action is to bring about a reduction in the level of violence that now exists.

It is to save the lives of brave men—and to save the lives of innocent women and children. It is to permit the contending forces to move closer to a political settlement. . . .

I call upon President Ho Chi Minh to respond positively, and favorably, to this new step toward peace.

But if peace does not come now through negotiations, it will come when Hanoi understands that our common resolve is unshakable, and our common strength is invincible.

Building a Durable South Vietnam

Tonight, we and the other allied nations are contributing 600,000 fighting men to assist 700,000 South Vietnamese troops in defending their little country.

Our presence there has always rested on this basic belief: The main burden of preserving their freedom must be carried out by them—by the South Vietnamese themselves.

We and our allies can only help to provide a shield behind which the people of South Vietnam can survive and can grow and develop. On their efforts—on their determination and resourcefulness the outcome will ultimately depend.

That small, beleaguered nation has suffered terrible punishment for more than 20 years.

I pay tribute once again tonight to the great courage and endurance of its people.

South Vietnam supports armed forces tonight of almost 700,000 men—and I call your attention to the fact that this is the equivalent of more than 10 million in our own population. Its people maintain their firm determination to be free of domination by the North.

There has been substantial progress, I think, in building a durable government during these last 3 years. The South Vietnam of 1965 could not have survived the enemy's Tet offensive of 1968. The elected government of South Vietnam survived that attack and is rapidly repairing the devastation that it wrought.

The South Vietnamese know that further efforts are going to be required:

- to expand their own armed forces,
- to move back into the countryside as quickly as possible,
- to increase their taxes,
- to select the very best men that they have for civil and military responsibility,
- to achieve a new unity within their constitutional government, and
- to include in the national effort all those groups who wish to preserve South Vietnam's control over its own destiny. . . .

President [Nguyen Van] Thieu told his people last week:

"We must make greater efforts and accept more sacrifices because, as I have said many times, this is our country. The existence of our nation is at stake, and this is mainly a Vietnamese responsibility."

He warned his people that a major national effort is required to root out corruption and incompetence at all levels of government.

We applaud this evidence of determination on the part of South Vietnam. Our first priority will be to support their effort.

We shall accelerate the reequipment of South Vietnam's armed forces—in order to meet the enemy's increased firepower. This will enable them progressively to undertake a larger share of combat operations against the Communist invaders. On many occasions I have told the American people that we would send to Vietnam those forces that are required to accomplish our mission there. So, with that as our guide, we have previously authorized a force level of approximately 525,000.

Some weeks ago—to help meet the enemy's new offensive—we sent to Vietnam about 11,000 additional Marine and airborne troops. They were deployed by air in 48 hours, on an emergency basis. But the artillery, tank, aircraft, medical, and other units that were needed to work with and to support these infantry troops in combat could not then accompany them by air on that short notice.

In order that these forces may reach maximum combat effectiveness, the Joint Chiefs of Staff have recommended to me that we should prepare to send—during the next 5 months—support troops totaling approximately 13,500 men.

A portion of these men will be made available from our active forces. The balance will come from reserve component units which will be called up for service. . . .

The Chances for Peace

Now let me give you my estimate of the chances for peace:
* the peace that will one day stop the bloodshed in South Vietnam,
* that will permit all the Vietnamese people to rebuild and develop their land,

• that will permit us to turn more fully to our own tasks here at home.

I cannot promise that the initiative that I have announced tonight will be completely successful in achieving peace any more than the 30 others that we have undertaken and agreed to in recent years.

But it is our fervent hope that North Vietnam, after years of fighting that have left the issue unresolved, will now cease its efforts to achieve a military victory and will join with us in moving toward the peace table.

And there may come a time when South Vietnamese—on both sides—are able to work out a way to settle their own differences by free political choice rather than by war.

As Hanoi considers its course, it should be in no doubt of our intentions. It must not miscalculate the pressures within our democracy in this election year.

We have no intention of widening this war.

But the United States will never accept a fake solution to this long and arduous struggle and call it peace.

No one can foretell the precise terms of an eventual settlement.

Our objective in South Vietnam has never been the annihilation of the enemy.

It has been to bring about a recognition in Hanoi that its objective—taking over the South by force—could not be achieved.

We think that peace can be based on the Geneva Accords of 1954—under political conditions that permit the South Vietnamese—all the South Vietnamese—to chart their course free of any outside domination or interference, from us or from anyone else.

So tonight I reaffirm the pledge that we made at Manila— that we are prepared to withdraw our forces from South Vietnam as the other side withdraws its forces to the north, stops the infiltration, and the level of violence thus subsides.

Our goal of peace and self-determination in Vietnam is directly related to the future of all of Southeast Asia—where much has happened to inspire confidence during the past 10 years. We have done all that we knew how to do to contribute and to help build that confidence.

A number of its nations have shown what can be accomplished under conditions of security. Since 1966, Indonesia, the fifth largest nation in all the world, with a population of more than 100 million people, has had a government that is dedicated to peace with its neighbors and improved conditions for its own people. Political and economic cooperation between nations has grown rapidly.

I think every American can take a great deal of pride in the role that we have played in bringing this about in Southeast Asia. We can rightly judge as responsible Southeast Asians themselves do—that the progress of the past 3 years would have been far less likely—if not completely impossible—if America's sons and others had not made their stand in Vietnam.

Peace Will Come

At Johns Hopkins University, about 3 years ago, I announced that the United States would take part in the great work of developing Southeast Asia, including the Mekong Valley, for all the people of that region. Our determination to help build a better land—a better land for men on both sides of the present conflict—has not diminished in the least. Indeed, the ravages of war, I think, have made it more urgent than ever.

So, I repeat on behalf of the United States again tonight what I said at Johns Hopkins—that North Vietnam could take its place in this common effort just as soon as peace comes.

Over time, a wider framework of peace and security in Southeast Asia may become possible. The new cooperation of the nations of the area could be a foundation-stone. Certainly friendship with the nations of such a Southeast Asia is what the United States seeks and that is all that the United States seeks.

One day, my fellow citizens, there will be peace in Southeast Asia.

It will come because the people of Southeast Asia want it—those whose armies are at war tonight, and those who, though threatened, have thus far been spared. Peace will come because Asians were willing to work for it—and to sacrifice for it—and to die by the thousands for it.

But let it never be forgotten: Peace will come also because America sent her sons to help secure it.

It has not been easy—far from it. During the past 4 1/2 years, it has been my fate and my responsibility to be Commander in Chief. I have lived—daily and nightly—with the cost of this war. I know the pain that it has inflicted. I know, perhaps better than anyone, the misgivings that it has aroused.

Throughout this entire, long period, I have been sustained by a single principle: that what we are doing now, in Vietnam, is vital not only to the security of Southeast Asia, but it is vital to the security of every American.

Surely we have treaties which we must respect. Surely we have commitments that we are going to keep. Resolutions of the Congress testify to the need to resist aggression in the world and in Southeast Asia.

But the heart of our involvement in South Vietnam—under three different Presidents, three separate administrations—has always been America's own security.

And the larger purpose of our involvement has always been to help the nations of Southeast Asia become independent and stand alone, self-sustaining, as members of a great world community—at peace with themselves, and at peace with all others.

With such an Asia, our country—and the world will be far more secure than it is tonight.

I believe that a peaceful Asia is far nearer to reality because of what America has done in Vietnam. I believe that the men who endure the dangers of battle fighting there for us tonight—are helping the entire world avoid far greater conflicts, far wider wars, far more destruction, than this one.

The peace that will bring them home someday will come. Tonight I have offered the first in what I hope will be a series of mutual moves toward peace.

I pray that it will not be rejected by the leaders of North Vietnam. I pray that they will accept it as a means by which the sacrifices of their own people may be ended. And I ask your help and your support, my fellow citizens, for this effort to reach across the battlefield toward an early peace.

Finally, my fellow Americans, let me say this:

Of those to whom much is given, much is asked. I cannot say and no man could say that no more will be asked of us.

Yet, I believe that now, no less than when the decade began, this generation of Americans is willing to "pay any price, bear any burden, meet any hardship, support any friend, oppose any foe to assure the survival and the success of liberty."

Since those words were spoken by John F. Kennedy, the people of America have kept that compact with mankind's noblest cause.

And we shall continue to keep it.

Yet, I believe that we must always be mindful of this one thing, whatever the trials and the tests ahead. The ultimate strength of our country and our cause will lie not in powerful weapons or infinite resources or boundless wealth, but will lie in the unity of our people.

This I believe very deeply.

Throughout my entire public career I have followed the personal philosophy that I am a free man, an American, a public servant, and a member of my party, in that order always and only.

For 37 years in the service of our Nation, first as a Congressman, as a Senator, and as Vice President, and now as your President, I have put the unity of the people first. I have put it ahead of any divisive partisanship.

And in these times as in times before, it is true that a house divided against itself by the spirit of faction, of party, of region, of religion, of race, is a house that cannot stand.

There is division in the American house now.

There is divisiveness among us all tonight. And holding the trust that is mine, as President of all the people, I cannot disregard the peril to the progress of the American people and the hope and the prospect of peace for all peoples.

So, I would ask all Americans, whatever their personal interests or concern, to guard against divisiveness and all its ugly consequences.

Fifty-two months and 10 days ago, in a moment of tragedy and trauma, the duties of this office fell upon me. I asked then for your help and God's, that we might continue America on its course, binding up our wounds, healing our history, moving forward in new unity, to clear the American agenda and to keep the American commitment for all of our people.

United we have kept that commitment. United we have enlarged that commitment.

Through all time to come, I think America will be a stronger nation, a more just society, and a land of greater opportunity and fulfillment because of what we have all done together in these years of unparalleled achievement.

Our reward will come in the life of freedom, peace, and hope that our children will enjoy through ages ahead.

What we won when all of our people united just must not now be lost in suspicion, distrust, selfishness, and politics among any of our people.

Renunciation

Believing this as I do, I have concluded that I should not permit the Presidency to become involved in the partisan divisions that are developing in this political year.

With America's sons in the fields far away, with America's future under challenge right here at home, with our hopes and the world's hopes for peace in the balance every day, I do not believe that I should devote an hour or a day of my time to any personal partisan causes or to any duties other than the awesome duties of this office—the Presidency of your country.

Accordingly, I shall not seek, and I will not accept, the nomination of my party for another term as your President.

But let men everywhere know, however, that a strong, a confident, and a vigilant America stands ready tonight to seek an honorable peace—and stands ready tonight to defend an honored cause whatever the price, whatever the burden, whatever the sacrifice that duty may require.

Americans Should Support the Vietnamization Plan for Ending the Vietnam War

Richard M. Nixon

By the time Richard M. Nixon became president in January 1969 on the promise of a secret plan to end the Vietnam War, his predecessor, Lyndon B. Johnson, had already stopped bombing North Vietnam and peace talks had begun in Paris, France. Nevertheless, U.S. troops in Vietnam still numbered more than five hundred forty thousand soldiers. On June 8, 1969, Nixon announced the withdrawal of twenty-five thousand U.S. troops and, on July 25, 1969, he announced the Nixon Doctrine, stating that the United States would honor its treaty commitments but would not bear the brunt of fighting in another country.

In a televised address to the nation on November 3, 1969, Nixon argues that the immediate withdrawal of U.S. troops would be a disaster. Instead, his Vietnamization Plan for ending the war includes gradually and methodically reducing U.S. combat forces in Vietnam, shifting military responsibilities to South Vietnamese forces, and continuing to negotiate for peace in Paris. Characterizing his antiwar critics as a vocal minority, Nixon asks for support for his plan from the silent majority of Americans.

Preceding this speech, on October 15, as many as

Excerpted from Richard M. Nixon's televised address to the American people, November 3, 1969.

1 million Americans had participated in the Moratorium, a nationwide suspension of work and school to protest the war. Another Moratorium, one that would become the largest American antiwar protest in history, was planned for November 15. With this speech, Nixon began a war against the antiwar movement, deepening the divisions in the American public and creating an internal turmoil and a vicious partisanship that would remain in American politics for years after his Vietnamization Plan had successfully ended American participation in the war.

Good evening, my fellow Americans:
Tonight I want to talk to you on a subject of deep concern to all Americans and to many people in all parts of the world—the war in Vietnam.

I believe that one of the reasons for the deep division about Vietnam is that many Americans have lost confidence in what their Government has told them about our policy. The American people cannot and should not be asked to support a policy which involves the overriding issues of war and peace unless they know the truth about that policy.

Tonight, therefore, I would like to answer some of the questions that I know are on the minds of many of you listening to me.

How and why did America get involved in Vietnam in the first place?

How has this administration changed the policy of the previous administration?

What has really happened in the negotiations in Paris and on the battlefront in Vietnam?

What choices do we have if we are to end the war?

What are the prospects for peace?

Now, let me begin by describing the situation I found when I was inaugurated on January 20.

The war had been going on for 4 years.

31,000 Americans had been killed in action.

The training program for the South Vietnamese was behind schedule.

540,000 Americans were in Vietnam with no plans to reduce the number.

No progress had been made at the negotiations in Paris
and the United States had not put forth a comprehensive
peace proposal.

The war was causing deep division at home and criticism
from many of our friends as well as our enemies abroad.

Some Urge Withdrawal

In view of these circumstances there were some who urged
that I end the war at once by ordering the immediate withdrawal of all American forces.

From a political standpoint this would have been a popular and easy course to follow. After all, we became involved
in the war while my predecessor was in office. I could blame
the defeat which would be the result of my action on him and
come out as the peacemaker. Some put it to me quite bluntly:
This was the only way to avoid allowing Johnson's war to
become Nixon's war.

But I had a greater obligation than to think only of the
years of my administration and of the next election. I had to
think of the effect of my decision on the next generation and
on the future of peace and freedom in America and in the
world.

Let us all understand that the question before us is not
whether some Americans are for peace and some Americans
are against peace. The question at issue is not whether Johnson's war becomes Nixon's war.

The great question is: How can we win America's peace?

Well, let us turn now to the fundamental issue. Why and
how did the United States become involved in Vietnam in the
first place?

Fifteen years ago North Vietnam, with the logistical support of Communist China and the Soviet Union, launched a
campaign to impose a Communist government on South
Vietnam by instigating and supporting a revolution.

In response to the request of the Government of South
Vietnam, President Eisenhower sent economic aid and military equipment to assist the people of South Vietnam in their

efforts to prevent a Communist takeover. Seven years ago, President Kennedy sent 16,000 military personnel to Vietnam as combat advisers. Four years ago, President Johnson sent American combat forces to South Vietnam.

Now, many believe that President Johnson's decision to send American combat forces to South Vietnam was wrong. And many others—I among them—have been strongly critical of the way the war has been conducted.

But the question facing us today is: Now that we are in the war, what is the best way to end it?

In January I could only conclude that the precipitate withdrawal of American forces from Vietnam would be a disaster not only for South Vietnam but for the United States and for the cause of peace.

For the South Vietnamese, our precipitate withdrawal would inevitably allow the Communists to repeat the massacres which followed their takeover in the North 15 years before. . . .

For the United States, this first defeat in our Nation's history would result in a collapse of confidence in American leadership, not only in Asia but throughout the world. . . .

For the future of peace, precipitate withdrawal would thus be a disaster of immense magnitude.

A nation cannot remain great if it betrays its allies and lets down its friends.

Our defeat and humiliation in South Vietnam without question would promote recklessness in the councils of those great powers who have not yet abandoned their goals of world conquest.

This would spark violence wherever our commitments help maintain the peace—in the Middle East, in Berlin, eventually even in the Western Hemisphere.

Ultimately, this would cost more lives.

It would not bring peace; it would bring more war.

For these reasons, I rejected the recommendation that I should end the war by immediately withdrawing all of our forces. I chose instead to change American policy on both the negotiating front and battlefront. . . .

It has become clear that the obstacle in negotiating an end to the war is not the President of the United States. And it is not the South Vietnamese.

The obstacle is the other side's absolute refusal to show the least willingness to join us in seeking a just peace. It will not do so while it is convinced that all it has to do is to wait for our next concession, and the next until it gets everything it wants.

There can now be no longer any question that progress in negotiation depends only on Hanoi's deciding to negotiate, to negotiate seriously.

I realize that this report on our efforts on the diplomatic fronts is discouraging to the American people, but the American people are entitled to know the truth—the bad news as well as the good news, where the lives of our young men are involved.

Now let me turn, however, to a more encouraging report on another front.

At the time we launched our search for peace I recognized we might not succeed in bringing an end to the war through negotiation. I, therefore, put into effect another plan to bring peace—a plan which will bring the war to an end regardless of what happens on the negotiating front.

The Nixon Doctrine

It is in line with a major shift in U.S. foreign policy which I described in my press conference at Guam on July 25. Let me briefly explain what has been described as the Nixon Doctrine—a policy which not only will help end the war in Vietnam, but which is an essential element of our program to prevent future Vietnams.

We Americans are a do-it-yourself-people. We are an impatient people. Instead of teaching someone else to do a job, we like to do it ourselves. And this trait has been carried over into our foreign policy.

In Korea and again in Vietnam, the United States furnished most of the money, most of the arms, and most of the men to help the people of those countries defend their freedom against the Communist aggression.

Before any American troops were committed to Vietnam, a leader of another Asian country expressed this opinion to me when I was traveling in Asia as a private citizen. He said, "When you are trying to assist another nation defend its freedom, U.S. policy should be to help them fight the war but not to fight the war for them."

Well, in accordance with this wise counsel, I laid down in Guam three principles as guidelines for future American policy toward Asia:

First, the United States will keep all of its treaty commitments.

Second, we shall provide a shield if a nuclear power threatens the freedom of a nation allied with us or of a nation whose survival we consider vital to our security.

Third, in cases involving other types of aggression, we shall furnish military and economic assistance when requested in accordance with our treaty commitments. But we shall look to the nation directly threatened to assume the primary responsibility of providing the manpower for its defense.

After I announced this policy, I found that the leaders of the Philippines, Thailand, Vietnam, South Korea, and other nations which might be threatened by Communist aggression, welcomed this new direction in American foreign policy.

Vietnamization

The defense of freedom is everybody's business—not just America's business. And it is particularly the responsibility of the people whose freedom is threatened. In the previous Administration, we Americanized the war in Vietnam. In this Administration, we are Vietnamizing the search for peace.

The policy of the previous Administration not only resulted in our assuming the primary responsibility for fighting the war but even more significantly did not adequately stress the goal of strengthening the South Vietnamese so that they could defend themselves when we left.

The Vietnamization Plan was launched following Secretary [of Defense Melvin] Laird's visit to Vietnam in March. Under the plan, I ordered first a substantial increase in the training and equipment of South Vietnamese forces.

In July, on my visit to Vietnam, I changed General [Creighton] Abrams' orders so that they were consistent with the objectives of our new policies. Under the new orders, the primary mission of our troops is to enable the South Vietnamese forces to assume the full responsibility for the security of South Vietnam.

Our air operations have been reduced by over 20 percent.

And now we have begun to see the results of this long overdue change in American policy in Vietnam.

Significant Results

After five years of Americans going into Vietnam, we are finally bringing American men home. By December 15, over 60,000 men will have been withdrawn from South Vietnam—including 20 percent of all of our combat forces.

The South Vietnamese have continued to gain in strength. As a result they have been able to take over combat responsibilities from our American troops.

Two other significant developments have occurred since this Administration took office.

Enemy infiltration, infiltration which is essential if they are to launch a major attack, over the last three months is less than 20 percent of what it was over the same period last year.

Most important—United States casualties have declined during the last two months to the lowest point in three years.

Let me now turn to our program for the future.

We have adopted a plan which we have worked out in cooperation with the South Vietnamese for the complete withdrawal of all U.S. combat ground forces, and their replacement by South Vietnamese forces on an orderly scheduled timetable. This withdrawal will be made from strength and not from weakness. As South Vietnamese forces become stronger, the rate of American withdrawal can become greater.

I have not and do not intend to announce the timetable for our program. There are obvious reasons for this decision which I am sure you will understand. As I have indicated on several occasions, the rate of withdrawal will depend on developments on three fronts.

One of these is the progress which can be or might be made in the Paris talks. An announcement of a fixed timetable for our withdrawal would completely remove any incentive for the enemy to negotiate an agreement.

They would simply wait until our forces had withdrawn and then move in.

The other two factors on which we will base our withdrawal decisions are the level of enemy activity and the progress of the training program of the South Vietnamese forces. I am glad to be able to report tonight progress on both of these fronts has been greater than we anticipated when we started the program in June for withdrawal. As a result, our timetable for withdrawal is more optimistic now than when we made our first estimates in June. This clearly demonstrates why it is not wise to be frozen in on a fixed timetable.

We must retain the flexibility to base each withdrawal decision on the situation as it is at that time rather than on estimates that are no longer valid.

Along with this optimistic estimate, I must—in all candor—leave one note of caution.

If the level of enemy activity significantly increases we might have to adjust our timetable accordingly.

However, I want the record to be completely clear on one point.

At the time of the bombing halt just a year ago, there was some confusion as to whether there was an understanding on the part of the enemy that if we stopped the bombing of North Vietnam they would stop the shelling of cities in South Vietnam. I want to be sure that there is no misunderstanding on the part of the enemy with regard to our withdrawal program.

We have noted the reduced level of infiltration, the reduction of our casualties, and are basing our withdrawal decisions partially on those factors.

If the level of infiltration or our casualties increase while we are trying to scale down the fighting, it will be the result of a conscious decision by the enemy.

Hanoi could make no greater mistake than to assume that an increase in violence will be to its advantage. If I conclude that increased enemy action jeopardizes our remaining forces in Vietnam, I shall not hesitate to take strong and effective measures to deal with that situation.

This is not a threat. This is a statement of policy which as Commander-in-Chief of our Armed Forces I am making in meeting my responsibility for the protection of American fighting men wherever they may be.

Two Choices

My fellow Americans, I am sure you recognize from what I have said that we really only have two choices open to us if we want to end this war.

I can order an immediate, precipitate withdrawal of all Americans from Vietnam without regard to the effects of that action.

Or we can persist in our search for a just peace through a negotiated settlement if possible, or through continued implementation of our plan for Vietnamization if necessary—a plan in which we will withdraw all our forces from Vietnam on a schedule in accordance with our program, as the South Vietnamese become strong enough to defend their own freedom.

I have chosen this second course.

It is not the easy way.

It is the right way.

It is a plan which will end the war and serve the cause of peace—not just in Vietnam but in the Pacific and in the world.

In speaking of the consequences of a precipitate withdrawal, I mentioned that our allies would lose confidence in America.

Far more dangerous, we would lose confidence in ourselves. Oh, the immediate reaction would be a sense of relief that our men were coming home. But as we saw the consequences of what we had done, inevitable remorse and divisive recrimination would scar our spirit as a people.

We have faced other crises in our history and have become stronger by rejecting the easy way out and taking the right way in meeting our challenges. Our greatness as a nation has been our capacity to do what had to be done when we knew our course was right.

Those Who Disagree

I recognize that some of my fellow citizens disagree with the plan for peace I have chosen. Honest and patriotic Americans have reached different conclusions as to how peace should be achieved.

In San Francisco a few weeks ago, I saw demonstrators carrying signs reading "Lose in Vietnam, bring the boys home."

Well, one of the strengths of our free society is that any American has a right to reach that conclusion and to advocate that point of view. But as President of the United States, I would be untrue to my oath of office if I allowed the policy of this Nation to be dictated by the minority who hold that point of view and who try to impose it on the Nation by mounting demonstrations in the street.

For almost 200 years, the policy of this Nation has been made under our Constitution by those leaders in the Congress and the White House elected by all of the people. If a vocal minority, however fervent its cause, prevails over reason and the will of the majority, this Nation has no future as a free society. . . .

And so tonight—to you, the great silent majority of my fellow Americans—I ask for your support.

I pledged in my campaign for the Presidency to end the war in a way that we could win the peace. I have initiated a plan of action which will enable me to keep that pledge.

The more support I can have from the American people, the sooner that pledge can be redeemed; for the more divided we are at home, the less likely the enemy is to negotiate at Paris.

Let us be united for peace. Let us also be united against defeat. Because let us understand: North Vietnam cannot defeat or humiliate the United States. Only Americans can do that.

Vietnam Veterans Call for Withdrawal from the Vietnam War

John Kerry

After graduating from Yale University, John Kerry enlisted in the navy in 1966 and served in the Vietnam War as an officer on a gunboat in the Mekong Delta. For his service in Vietnam, Kerry earned a Silver Star, a Bronze Star, three Purple Hearts, two Presidential Unit Citations, and a National Defense Service medal. When Kerry returned home, he became a social activist for Vietnam veterans, cofounder of the Vietnam Veterans of America, and leader of Vietnam Veterans Against the War (VVAW), an organization of Vietnam veterans formed in June 1967 to protest the war.

On April 22, 1971, Kerry testified on behalf of the Vietnam Veterans Against the War before Senator J. William Fulbright's Senate Foreign Relations Committee. Speaking less than a month after Lieutenant William Calley had been convicted of murdering civilians at the My Lai massacre, Kerry talks about atrocities that U.S. soldiers confessed during the Winter Soldier Investigation that veterans had conducted themselves a few months earlier. He characterizes the war as a civil war by a people who want liberation from colonial influence and do not know the difference between communism and democracy. Kerry praises the antiwar protestors that Vice President Spiro Agnew called "criminal misfits" and joins them in calling for an

Excerpted from John Kerry's statement before the United States Senate Committee on Foreign Relations, April 22, 1971.

immediate American withdrawal from Vietnam, asking, "How do you ask a man to be the last man to die in Vietnam? How do you ask a man to die for a mistake?"

After the war, Kerry continued to champion Vietnam veterans and the Vietnamese people as a United States senator. As a member of the Senate Foreign Relations Committee, he advocated normalizing relations with Vietnam. In November 2000, Kerry accompanied President Bill Clinton to Hanoi for the president's speech at Vietnam National University, and he helped pass an agreement normalizing trade with Vietnam less than a year later.

I would like to say for the record, and also for the men behind me who are also wearing the uniform and their medals, that my sitting here is really symbolic. I am not here as John Kerry. I am here as one member of the group of 1,000 which is a small representation of a very much larger group of veterans in this country, and were it possible for all of them to sit at this table they would be here and have the same kind of testimony. . . .

I would like to talk on behalf of all those veterans and say that several months ago in Detroit we had an investigation at which over 150 honorably discharged, and many very highly decorated, veterans testified to war crimes committed in Southeast Asia. These were not isolated incidents but crimes committed on a day to day basis with the full awareness of officers at all levels of command.

It is impossible to describe to you exactly what did happen in Detroit—the emotions in the room and the feelings of the men who were reliving their experiences in Vietnam. They relived the absolute horror of what this country, in a sense, made them do.

Stories of Atrocities

They told stories that at times they had personally raped, cut off ears, cut off heads, taped wires from portable telephones to human genitals and turned up the power, cut off limbs, blown up bodies, randomly shot at civilians, razed villages in fashion reminiscent of Genghis Khan, shot cattle and dogs for fun, poisoned food stocks, and generally ravaged the countryside of South Vietnam in addition to the normal ravage of war and the normal and very particular ravaging which is done by the applied bombing power of this country.

We call this investigation the Winter Soldier Investigation. The term Winter Soldier is a play on words of Thomas Paine's in 1776 when he spoke of the Sunshine Patriots and summer time soldiers who deserted at Valley Forge because the going was rough.

We who have come here to Washington have come here because we feel we have to be winter soldiers now. We could come back to this country, we could be quiet, we could hold our silence, we could not tell what went on in Vietnam, but we feel because of what threatens this country, not the reds, but the crimes which we are committing that threaten it, that we have to speak out.

I would like to talk to you a little bit about what the result is of the feelings these men carry with them after coming back from Vietnam. The country doesn't know it yet but it has created a monster, a monster in the form of millions of men who have been taught to deal and to trade in violence and who are given the chance to die for the biggest nothing in history; men who have returned with a sense of anger and a sense of betrayal which no one has yet grasped.

As a veteran and one who feels this anger I would like to talk about it. We are angry because we feel we have been used in the worst fashion by the administration of this country.

In 1970 at West Point Vice President [Spiro T.] Agnew said "some glamorize the criminal misfits of society while our best men die in Asian rice paddies to preserve the freedom which most of those misfits abuse," and this was used as a rallying point for our effort in Vietnam.

But for us, as boys in Asia whom the country was supposed to support, his statement is a terrible distortion from which we can only draw a very deep sense of revulsion, and hence the anger of some of the men who are here in Washington today. It is a distortion because we in no way consider ourselves the best men of this country; because those he calls misfits were standing up for us in a way that nobody else in this country dared to; because so many who have died would have returned to this country to join the misfits in their efforts to ask for an immediate withdrawal from South Vietnam; because so many of those best men have returned as quadriplegics and amputees—and they lie forgotten in Veterans Administration Hospitals in this country which fly the flag which so many have chosen as their own personal symbol—and we cannot consider ourselves America's best men when we are ashamed of and hated for what we were called on to do in Southeast Asia.

In our opinion, and from our experience, there is nothing in South Vietnam which could happen that realistically threatens the United States of America. And to attempt to justify the loss of one American life in Vietnam, Cambodia or Laos by linking such loss to the preservation of freedom, which those misfits supposedly abuse, is to us the height of criminal hypocrisy, and it is that kind of hypocrisy which we feel has torn this country apart.

We are probably much more angry than that, but I don't want to go into the foreign policy aspects because I am outclassed here. I know that all of you talk about every possible alternative for getting out of Vietnam. We understand that. We know you have considered the seriousness of the aspects to the utmost level and I am not going to try to dwell on that. But I want to relate to you the feeling that many of the men who have returned to this country express because we are probably angriest about all that we were told about Vietnam and about the mystical war against communism.

What We Saw

We found that not only was it a civil war, an effort by a people who had for years been seeking their liberation from any colonial influence whatsoever, but also we found that the Vietnamese whom we had enthusiastically molded after our own image were hard put to take up the fight against the threat we were supposedly saving them from.

We found most people didn't even know the difference between communism and democracy. They only wanted to work in rice paddies without helicopters strafing them and bombs with napalm burning their villages and tearing their country apart. They wanted everything to do with the war, particularly with this foreign presence of the United States of America, to leave them alone in peace, and they practiced the art of survival by siding with whichever military force was present at a particular time, be it Viet Cong, North Vietnamese or American.

Many people protested the draft because of the atrocities committed by some of those who went to Vietnam.

We found also that all too often American men were dying in those rice paddies for want of support from their allies. We saw firsthand how monies from American taxes were used for a corrupt dictatorial regime. We saw that many people in this country had a one-sided idea of who was kept free by our flag, and blacks provided the highest percentage of casualties. We saw Vietnam ravaged equally by American bombs and search and destroy missions, as well as by Viet Cong terrorism, and yet we listened while this country tried to blame all of the havoc on the Viet Cong.

We rationalized destroying villages in order to save them. We saw America lose her sense of morality as she accepted very coolly a My Lai [where U.S. troops murdered hundreds of Vietnamese civilians] and refused to give up the image of American soldiers who hand out chocolate bars and chewing gum.

We learned the meaning of free fire zones, shooting anything that moves, and we watched while America placed a
cheapness on the lives of orientals.

We watched the United States falsification of body
counts, in fact the glorification of body counts. We listened
while month after month we were told the back of the enemy
was about to break. We fought using weapons against "ori-
ental human beings." We fought using weapons against those
people which I do not believe this country would dream of
using were we fighting in the European theater. We watched
while men charged up hills because a general said that hill
has to be taken, and after losing one platoon or two platoons
they marched away to leave the hill for reoccupation by the
North Vietnamese. We watched pride allow the most unim-
portant battles to be blown into extravaganzas, because we
couldn't lose, and we couldn't retreat, and because it didn't
matter how many American bodies were lost to prove that
point, and so there were Hamburger Hills and Khe Sanhs
and Hill 81s and Fire Base 6s, and so many others. Now we
are told that the men who fought there must watch quietly
while American lives are lost so that we can exercise the in-
credible arrogance of Vietnamizing the Vietnamese.

Each day to facilitate the process by which the United
States washes her hands of Vietnam someone has to give up
his life so that the United States doesn't have to admit something that the entire world already knows, so that we can't
say that we have made a mistake. Someone has to die so that
President Nixon won't be, and these are his words, "the first
President to lose a war."

To Die for a Mistake

We are asking Americans to think about that because how do
you ask a man to be the last man to die in Vietnam? How do
you ask a man to be the last man to die for a mistake? But
we are trying to do that, and we see doing it with thousands
of rationalizations, and if you read carefully the President's
last speech to the people of this country, you can see that he
says, and says clearly:

But the issue, gentlemen, the issue is communism, and the

question is whether or not we will leave that country to the Communists or whether or not we will try to give it hope to be a free people.

But the point is they are not a free people now under us. They are not a free people, and we cannot fight communism all over the world, and I think we should have learned that lesson by now. . . .

We are asking here in Washington for some action; action from the Congress of the United States of America which has the power to raise and maintain armies, and which by the Constitution also has the power to declare war.

We have come here, not to the President, because we believe that this body can be responsive to the will of the people, and we believe that the will of the people says that we should be out of Vietnam now.

We are here in Washington also to say that the problem of this war is not just a question of war and diplomacy. It is part and parcel of everything that we are trying as human beings to communicate to people in this country—the question of racism which is rampant in the military, and so many other questions such as the use of weapons; the hypocrisy of our taking umbrage at the Geneva Conventions and using that as justification for a continuation of this war when we are more guilty than any other body of violations of those Geneva Conventions; in the use of free fire zones, harassment interdiction fire, search and destroy missions, the bombings, the torture of prisoners, the killing of prisoners, all accepted policy by many units in South Vietnam. That is what we are trying to say. It is part and parcel of everything.

An American Indian friend of mine who lives in the Indian Nation of Alcatraz put it to me very succinctly. He told me how as a boy on an Indian reservation he had watched television and he used to cheer the cowboys when they came in and shot the Indians, and then suddenly one day he stopped in Vietnam and he said, "My God, I am doing to these people the very same thing that was done to my people," and he stopped. And that is what we are trying to say, that we think this thing has to end.

We are also here to ask, and we are here to ask vehemently,

where are the leaders of our country? Where is the leadership? We are here to ask where are [Robert] McNamara, [Walt] Rostow, [McGeorge] Bundy, [Roswell] Gilpatric and so many others? Where are they now that we, the men whom they sent off to war, have returned? These are commanders who have deserted their troops, and there is no more serious crime in the laws of war. The Army says they never leave their wounded. The Marines say they never leave even their dead. These men have left the real stuff of their reputation bleaching behind them in the sun in this country.

Finally, this administration has done us the ultimate dishonor. They have attempted to disown us and the sacrifices we made for this country. In their blindness and fear they have tried to deny that we are veterans or that we served in Nam. We do not need their testimony. Our own scars and stumps or limbs are witness enough for others and for ourselves.

We wish that a merciful God could wipe away our own memories of that service as easily as this administration has wiped away the memories of us. But all that they have done and all that they can do by this denial is to make more clear than ever our own determination to undertake one less mission—to search out and destroy the last vestige of this barbaric war, to pacify our hearts, to conquer the hate and the fear that have driven this country these last ten years and more, so when 30 years from now our brothers go down the street without a leg, without an arm, or a face, and small boys ask why, we will be able to say "Vietnam" and not mean a desert, not a filthy obscene memory, but mean instead the place where America finally turned and where soldiers like us helped it in the turning.

The United States Is Bringing Peace with Honor to Vietnam

Richard M. Nixon

While campaigning for the U.S. presidency in 1968,
Richard M. Nixon learned that President Lyndon B.
Johnson's negotiators had reached an agreement with
North Vietnam in the Paris peace talks. After a briefing
by Secretary of State Dean Rusk about the agreement,
Nixon, fearing that a peace agreement by the Johnson ad-
mininistration might help Vice President Hubert
Humphrey win the presidential election, secretly contacted South Vietnamese leaders and advised them to
hold out for a better deal from the Nixon administration,
effectively sabotaging peace negotiations.

After becoming president, Nixon, adopting National
Security Adviser Henry Kissinger's strategy of using military strength to force opponents to bargain for peace,
continued peace negotiations while escalating the war by
bombing North Vietnam and North Vietnamese sanctuaries in Cambodia, sending U.S. troops into Cambodia, and
mining North Vietnamese harbors. In addition, he visited
China and the Soviet Union in 1972 to ease relationships
with North Vietnam's allies. When Kissinger and North
Vietnamese negotiator Le Duc Tho reached a cease-fire
agreement in October, just before the 1972 presidential
elections, Nixon, reluctant to appear to be making peace
simply to win the election, rejected it. When peace talks
stalled, Nixon ordered the greatest air attacks of the war

Excerpted from Richard M. Nixon's televised address to the American people,
January 23, 1973.

on North Vietnam in December 1972. Peace talks resumed in January 1973.

In the following televised address to the nation on January 23, 1973, President Nixon announces that the United States and North Vietnam have finally negotiated "peace with honor" in Vietnam. Four days later, on January 27, 1973, U.S. participation in the Vietnam War ended with the signing of the Paris Peace Accords. North Vietnam began releasing American prisoners of war and, with the release of the final sixty-seven prisoners of war on March 29, 1973, the last U.S. combat troops left Vietnam. Postwar analysis of the Nixon-Kissinger strategy revealed that the United States had underestimated the determination of the Vietnamese people and that Nixon's terroristic bombing of Hanoi had gained U.S. negotiators virtually no advantage while costing the U.S. government considerable prestige and credibility in the international community and at home. Nixon and Kissinger finally negotiated a way for the United States to leave Vietnam without conceding defeat by yielding more to North Vietnamese negotiators in each talk until the final agreement, which essentially yielded South Vietnam to the Communists. On April 30, 1975, the last Americans in Vietnam left by helicopters from the roof of the U.S. embassy in Saigon as the Communists took over South Vietnam and finally ended the Vietnam War.

I have asked for this radio and television time tonight for the purpose of announcing that we today have concluded an agreement to end the war and bring peace with honor in Vietnam and in Southeast Asia.

The following statement is being issued at this moment in Washington and Hanoi:

At 12:30 Paris time today [Tuesday], January 23, 1973, the Agreement on Ending the War and Restoring Peace in Vietnam was initialed by Dr. Henry Kissinger on behalf of the United States, and Special Adviser Le Duc Tho on behalf of the Democratic Republic of Vietnam.

The agreement will be formally signed by the parties participating in the Paris Conference on Vietnam on January 27, 1973, at the International Conference Center in Paris.

The cease-fire will take effect at 2400 Greenwich Mean Time, January 27, 1973. The United States and the Democratic Republic of Vietnam express the hope that this agreement will insure stable peace in Vietnam and contribute to the preservation of lasting peace in Indochina and Southeast Asia.

That concludes the formal statement.

Throughout the years of negotiations, we have insisted on peace with honor. In my addresses to the Nation from this room of January 25 and May 8, [1972] I set forth the goals that we considered essential for peace with honor.

In the settlement that has now been agreed to, all the conditions that I laid down then have been met. A cease-fire, internationally supervised, will begin at 7 p.m., this Saturday, January 27, Washington time. Within 60 days from this Saturday, all Americans held prisoners of war throughout Indochina will be released. There will be the fullest possible accounting for all of those who are missing in action.

During the same 60-day period, all American forces will be withdrawn from South Vietnam.

The people of South Vietnam have been guaranteed the right to determine their own future, without outside interference.

By joint agreement, the full text of the agreement and the protocols to carry it out, will be issued tomorrow. Throughout these negotiations we have been in the closest consultation with President [Nguyen Van] Thieu and other representatives of the Republic of Vietnam. This settlement meets the goals and has the full support of President Thieu and the Government of the Republic of Vietnam, as well as that of our other allies who are affected.

The United States will continue to recognize the Government of the Republic of Vietnam as the sole legitimate government of South Vietnam.

We shall continue to aid South Vietnam within the terms of the agreement and we shall support efforts by the people of South Vietnam to settle their problems peacefully among themselves.

We must recognize that ending the war is only the first step toward building the peace. All parties must now see to it that this is a peace that lasts, and also a peace that heals, and a peace that not only ends the war in Southeast Asia, but contributes to the prospects of peace in the whole world.

This will mean that the terms of the agreement must be scrupulously adhered to. We shall do everything the agreement requires of us and we shall expect the other parties to do everything it requires of them. We shall also expect other interested nations to help ensure that the agreement is carried out and peace is maintained. As this long and very difficult war ends, I would like to address a few special words to each of those who have been parties in the conflict.

First, to the people and Government of South Vietnam: By your courage, by your sacrifice, you have won the precious right to determine your own future and you have developed the strength to defend that right. We look forward to working with you in the future, friends in peace as we have been allies in war.

To the leaders of North Vietnam: As we have ended the war through negotiations, let us now build a peace of reconciliation. For our part; we are prepared to make a major effort to help achieve that goal. But just as reciprocity was needed to end the war, so, too, will it be needed to build and strengthen the peace.

To the other major powers that have been involved even indirectly: Now is the time for mutual restraint so that the peace we have achieved can last.

And finally, to all of you who are listening, the American people: Your steadfastness in supporting our insistence on peace with honor has made peace with honor possible. I know that you would not have wanted that peace jeopardized. With our secret negotiations at the sensitive stage they were in during this recent period, for me to have discussed publicly our efforts to secure peace would not only have violated our understanding with North Vietnam, it would have seriously harmed and possibly destroyed the chances for peace. Therefore, I know that you now can understand why, during these past several weeks, I have not made any public statements about those efforts.

The important thing was not to talk about peace, but to get peace and to get the right kind of peace. This we have done.

Now that we have achieved an honorable agreement, let us be proud that America did not settle for a peace that would have betrayed our allies, that would have abandoned our prisoners of war, or that would have ended the war for us but would have continued the war for the 50 million people of Indochina. Let us be proud of the 2½ million young Americans who served in Vietnam, who served with honor and distinction in one of the most selfless enterprises in the history of nations. And let us be proud of those who sacrificed, who gave their lives so that the people of South Vietnam might live in freedom and so that the world might live in peace.

In particular, I would like to say a word to some of the bravest people I have ever met—the wives, the children, the families of our prisoners of war and the missing in action. When others called on us to settle on any terms, you had the courage to stand for the right kind of peace so that those who died and those who suffered would not have died and suffered in vain, and so that, where this generation knew war, the next generation would know peace. Nothing means more to me at this moment than the fact that your long vigil is coming to an end.

Just yesterday, a great American, who once occupied this office, died. In his life President [Lyndon B.] Johnson endured the vilification of those who sought to portray him as a man of war. But there was nothing he cared about more deeply than achieving a lasting peace in the world.

I remember the last time I talked with him. It was just the day after New Year's. He spoke then of his concern with bringing peace, with making it the right kind of peace, and I was grateful that he once again expressed his support for my efforts to gain such a peace. No one would have welcomed this peace more than he.

And I know he would join me in asking for those who died and for those who live, let us consecrate this moment by resolving together to make the peace we have achieved a peace that will last.

CHAPTER
SIX

GREAT
SPEECHES
IN
HISTORY

Postwar
Legacy

The Invisible Vietnam Veteran

James H. Webb

After graduating from the U.S. Naval Academy in Annapolis in 1968, James H. Webb served in the Fifth Marine Regiment in Vietnam, eventually earning the Navy Cross, a Silver Star Medal, two Bronze Stars, and two Purple Hearts. After the war, Webb worked as a lawyer helping Vietnam veterans with legal problems. For his work, the Vietnam Veterans Civic Council named him the "Outstanding Veteran" for 1976.

Webb later served as counsel to the House Committee on Veterans Affairs before becoming U.S secretary of the navy in 1987. He has written several novels and produced films about his experience in Vietnam.

In the following acceptance speech on August 4, 1976, Webb expresses the bitterness of Vietnam veterans who returned home to a hostile American public and an unsympathetic American government. He shares his hope that receiving this award will confer some much deserved dignity and respect on his fellow veterans. The issue that Webb mentions of whether to grant amnesty to American men who had evaded the draft was generating controversy at the time of this speech during the 1976 presidential campaign. President Jimmy Carter would pardon most of the ten thousand Vietnam War draft evaders on January 21, 1977, the day after his inauguration.

The most important part of an award such as this is its symbolic value as notice to the community. I don't need to elaborate in front of this assemblage about how incredibly difficult it has been for the Vietnam veteran. His anonymity and lack of positive feedback about himself and his fellow veterans have intensified all the other difficulties he has faced, including those shared by non-veterans. With the exception of a few well-publicized disaster stories, he is invisible.

To my mind, the roots of this problem go back 10 and 11 years, when the veteran suffered the irony of having people who directly opposed both his views and his acts become accepted as his spokesmen, in the name of the "generation gap," since he and they were from the same age group. But it's obvious that it wasn't age that separated views on Vietnam, and especially on what to do about it. It was culture. And the cultures that fought Vietnam have traditionally lacked access to the media and power centers of this country. As a result, their views have gone unheard and it has been presumed that, on the whole, "youth" embraced the views of the anti-war faction.

The lack of positive feedback persists. A Vietnam veteran looks for success stories within his own age group and finds that, by and large, they belong to people from one of two subgroups. Either the person managed to avoid the war altogether, with no stigma for doing so, and was able to devote full time to his field without the interruption of being in the service, or he actively opposed the war and has now converted his anti-war activities into credentials—much as the veteran of World War II did with his campaign ribbons.

The anonymity persists. I recall my most frustrating moment as a Vietnam veteran. The day after Saigon fell and it was finally over, a local newspaper ran what was tantamount to a special edition on "What Vietnam Did To America." On the front page were two human-interest stories. One detailed the frustrations of a draft resister. The other was about a person who had quit his civil service job because he had "lost faith" in the American system of government, and then sadly, had to become a lawyer. The center of the front section had two full pages of interviews—at least 50 of them—with people from across the entire spectrum of American cultures.

With one exception. There was not one interview with a Vietnam veteran. It was as if he had ceased to exist along with the government of South Vietnam—or perhaps was merely considered irrelevant in determining the effect on the rest of society of the very issue that had touched him the most directly and intensely.

And the whole notion of invisibility persists in other forms as well. We read repeated editorials and articles urging amnesty for the ones who fled. I realize that there is much room for differences of opinion on the issue, even among veterans. But no matter what a Vietnam veteran's position on the amnesty issue, he cannot help but feel the knife twist every time he reads articles that evaluate the ones who fled, collectively, to the level of prophets and moral purists. The phrase that sticks on my mind, used quite often, is that they "obeyed a higher law, that of their own conscience, and fled."

The unwritten implication, again and again, is that the Vietnam veteran, who merely obeyed the "lower law," that of his country, did so out of immorality or lack of conscience. Or, to be blunt, we seem to have reached the anomaly where the very institution, and the same newspaper, who only a few years ago called for us to bleed, have now decided that we should be ashamed of our scars.

Well, I'm not ashamed of mine. And I will always believe that the individual who agonized over the incredibly complex moral and political issue of Vietnam and then went there, displayed an equal level of conscience, and a hell of a lot more maturity, than his counterpart who fled. To go required an acceptance, sometimes conscious and sometimes visceral, of the premise that he was living in a nation of laws and not specially privileged people. It also required a sublimation of self to what, at least to them, was perceived to be in the public good. The person who fled, no matter how great his agonizings, finally decided the issue in his own self-interest. If he had been a true "moral purist," he would have gone to jail for his beliefs.

The Vietnam veteran has a lot to be proud of. If the anti-war elements in this country had opposed the war with the same maturity and patience that he displayed in fighting it, perhaps 10,000 more of his contemporaries might be alive today. People being what they are, and emotions what they are, Vietnam would have been a less volatile issue, and the war would have ended sooner.

I earnestly hope that awards such as this will encourage the community to accord the Vietnam veteran with dignity and respect. He has always deserved it.

The Unknown Soldier of the Vietnam War

Ronald Reagan

After attracting national attention with a television address supporting Barry Goldwater's 1964 presidential campaign against Lyndon Johnson, Ronald Reagan won the California gubernatorial election with campaign speeches criticizing the student antiwar movement. As governor, he fired the president of the University of California in Berkeley for being too lenient with student demonstrators and reduced state funding of universities where students protested against the Vietnam War. After Reagan became president in 1981, the United States began to acknowledge the service of Vietnam War veterans with the dedication in Washington, D.C., on November 11, 1982, of the Vietnam Veterans Memorial, a black granite wall stretching 492 feet and holding the names of every American soldier who died in the Vietnam War.

Speaking at the Arlington National Cemetery on May 28, 1984, President Reagan presents the Congressional Medal of Honor, the most prestigious military award in the United States, to the Unknown Soldier of the Vietnam War. Referring to the recent dedication of the Vietnam Veterans Memorial, Reagan suggests that the United States is finally ready to honor veterans of the Vietnam War who had not received a hero's welcome at the end of the war. He claims the lesson of Vietnam is that government should seek public support by explaining its actions, and he cautions that the war is not over for families of soldiers still missing.

Excerpted from Ronald Reagan's remarks at Memorial Day Ceremonies Honoring an Unknown Serviceman of the Vietnam Conflict, May 28, 1984.

At the end of the Vietnam War, over twenty-five hundred soldiers were still missing-in-action (MIA), and some
Americans suspected that Communist forces continued to
hold American prisoners of war (POWs). President
Jimmy Carter had started negotiations to normalize relations with Vietnam in exchange for a fuller accounting
for POW/MIAs, but negotiations had failed. The
POW/MIA issue would continue to block relations with
Vietnam for the remainder of the century.

Memorial Day is a day of ceremonies and speeches.
Throughout America today, we honor the dead of
our wars. We recall their valor and their sacrifices.
We remember they gave their lives so that others might live.

We're also gathered here for a special event—the national
funeral for an unknown soldier who will today join the heroes of three other wars.

When he spoke at a ceremony at Gettysburg in 1863,
President [Abraham] Lincoln reminded us that through their
deeds, the dead had spoken more eloquently for themselves
than any of the living ever could, and that we living could
only honor them by rededicating ourselves to the cause for
which they so willingly gave a last full measure of devotion.

Well, this is especially so today, for in our minds and
hearts is the memory of Vietnam and all that that conflict
meant for those who sacrificed on the field of battle and for
their loved ones who suffered here at home.

Not long ago, when a memorial was dedicated here in
Washington to our Vietnam veterans, the events surrounding
that dedication were a stirring reminder of America's re-
silience, of how our nation could learn and grow and transcend the tragedies of the past.

During the dedication ceremonies, the rolls of those who
died and are still missing were read for 3 days in a candlelight
ceremony at the National Cathedral. And the veterans of
Vietnam who were never welcomed home with speeches and
bands, but who were never defeated in battle and were heroes
as surely as any who have ever fought in a noble cause, staged

their own parade on Constitution Avenue [in Washington, D.C.]. As America watched them—some in wheelchairs, all of them proud—there was a feeling that this nation—that as a nation we were coming together again and that we had, at long last, welcomed the boys home. . . .

We Americans have learned to listen to each other and to trust each other again. We've learned that government owes the people an explanation and needs their support for its actions at home and abroad. And we have learned, and I pray this time for good, the most valuable lesson of all—the preciousness of human freedom.

It has been a lesson relearned not just by Americans but by all the people of the world. Yet, while the experience of Vietnam has given us a stark lesson that ultimately must move the conscience of the world, we must remember that we cannot today, as much as some might want to, close this chapter in our history, for the war in Southeast Asia still haunts a small but brave group of Americans—the families of those still missing in the Vietnam conflict.

They live day and night with uncertainty, with an emptiness, with a void that we cannot fathom. Today some sit among you. Their feelings are a mixture of pride and fear. They're proud of their sons or husbands, fathers or brothers who bravely and nobly answered the call of their country. But some of them fear that this ceremony writes a final chapter, leaving those they love forgotten.

Well, today then, one way to honor those who served or may still be serving in Vietnam is to gather here and rededicate ourselves to securing the answers for the families of those missing in action. I ask the Members of Congress, the leaders of veterans groups, and the citizens of an entire nation present or listening, to give these families your help and your support, for they still sacrifice and suffer.

Vietnam is not over for them. They cannot rest until they know the fate of those they loved and watched march off to serve their country. Our dedication to their cause must be strengthened with these events today. We write no last chapters. We close no books. We put away no final memories. An end to America's involvement in Vietnam cannot come before we've achieved the fullest possible accounting of those missing in action.

This can only happen when their families know with certainty that this nation discharged her duty to those who served nobly and well. Today a united people call upon Hanoi with one voice: Heal the sorest wound of this conflict. Return our sons to America. End the grief of those who are innocent and undeserving of any retribution.

The Unknown Soldier who is returned to us today and whom we lay to rest is symbolic of all our missing sons, and we will present him with the Congressional Medal of Honor, the highest military decoration that we can bestow.

About him we may well wonder, as others have: As a child, did he play on some street in a great American city? Or did he work beside his father on a farm out in America's heartland? Did he marry? Did he have children? Did he look expectantly to return to a bride?

We'll never know the answers to these questions about his life. We do know, though, why he died. He saw the horrors of war but bravely faced them, certain his own cause and his country's cause was a noble one; that he was fighting for human dignity, for free men everywhere. Today we pause to embrace him and all who served us so well in a war whose end offered no parades, no flags, and so little thanks. We can be worthy of the values and ideals for which our sons sacrificed—worthy of their courage in the face of a fear that few of us will ever experience—by honoring their commitment and devotion to duty and country.

Many veterans of Vietnam still serve in the Armed Forces, work in our offices, on our farms, and in our factories. Most have kept their experiences private, but most have been strengthened by their call to duty. A grateful nation opens her heart today in gratitude for their sacrifice, for their courage, and for their noble service. Let us, if we must, debate the lessons learned at some other time. Today, we simply say with pride, "Thank you, dear son. May God cradle you in His loving arms."

We present to you our nation's highest award, the Congressional Medal of Honor, for service above and beyond the call of duty in action with the enemy during the Vietnam era.

Foreign Policy Lessons of the Vietnam War

George P. Shultz

During the Vietnam War, George P. Shultz served under President Richard Nixon, first as secretary of labor in 1969, then as director of the Office of Management and Budget, and finally as the secretary of the treasury between 1972 and 1974. On July 16, 1982, Shultz became the U.S. secretary of state under President Ronald Reagan.

In his speech at the Department of State on the tenth anniversary of the fall of South Vietnam to North Vietnamese forces, Schultz details the history of Indochina since 1975, discussing the moral issues and the strategic price of American withdrawal from the Vietnam War. Decrying American foreign policy weakness, he criticizes restraints on the president, such as the War Powers Resolution, which Congress passed in November 1973 to rescind the Gulf of Tonkin Resolution and which requires the president to seek congressional approval for military deployments. After reflecting on the illusions of the Vietnam period, he concludes that world stability requires the United States to accept the role of advancing the cause of freedom.

T he 10th anniversary of the fall of Indochina is an occasion for all of us, as a nation, to reflect on the meaning of that experience. As the fierce emotions of that time subside, perhaps our country has a better chance now of

Excerpted from George P. Shultz's speech at the Department of State, April 25, 1985.

assessing the war and its impact. This is not merely a historical exercise. Our understanding of the past affects our conduct in the present, and thus, in part, determines our future.

Let me discuss what has happened in Southeast Asia, and
the world, since 1975; what light those postwar events shed
on the war itself; and what relevance all this has to our foreign policy today.

Indochina Since 1975

The first point—and it stands out for all to see—is that the
communist subjection of Indochina has fulfilled the worst
predictions of the time. The bloodshed and misery that communist rule wrought in South Vietnam, and in Cambodia
and Laos, add yet another grim chapter to the catalog of
agony of the 20th century.

Since 1975, over 1 million refugees have fled South Vietnam to escape the new tyranny. In 1978, Hanoi decided to encourage the flight of refugees by boat. At its height in the
spring of 1979, the exodus of these "boat people" reached
over 40,000 a month. Tens, perhaps hundreds, of thousands
never made it to safety and today lie beneath the South China
Sea. Others managed to survive pirate attacks and other hard-
ships at sea in their journey to freedom. We have welcomed
more than 730,000 Indochinese refugees to our shores. . . .

When the North Vietnamese Army conquered the south,
it rounded up officials and supporters of the South Vietnamese Government, as well as other suspected opponents.
Many were executed or disappeared forever. . . . To this day,
upward of 10,000 remain imprisoned. They include Buddhist
and Christian clergy and intellectuals, as well as former political figures. According to refugee reports, they face inde-
terminate sentences, receive food rations below subsistence
levels, are denied basic medical care, and are punished severely for even minor infractions of camp rules—punishment
often resulting in permanent injury or death.

Hanoi has asserted for years that it will let these prisoners go if only we would take them all. Last fall, President
[Ronald] Reagan offered to bring all genuine political prisoners to freedom in the United States. Now, Hanoi no longer

adheres to its original proposal. . . .

Compare conditions in Vietnam under 10 years of communist rule with conditions in the South Vietnam we fought to defend. The South Vietnamese Government accepted the principles of free elections, freedom of speech, of the press, and of association. From 1967 to 1971 the South Vietnamese people voted in nine elections; opposition parties played a major role in the assembly. Before 1975 there were 27 daily newspapers, some 200 journals of opinion and scholarship, 3 television and 2 dozen radio stations, all operating in relative freedom.

No, South Vietnam was not a Jeffersonian democracy with full civil liberties by American standards. But there was a vigorous, pluralist political process, and the government intruded little into the private lives of the people. They enjoyed religious freedom and ethnic tolerance, and there were few restrictions on cultural or intellectual life. The transgressions of the [Nguyen Van] Thieu government pale into insignificance next to the systematic, ideologically impelled despotism of the regime that replaced it.

The neutralist government in neighboring Laos was swiftly taken over in 1975 by local communists loyal to Hanoi. As in Vietnam, thousands of former officials were sent to "reeducation camps." Fifty thousand Vietnamese troops remain in Laos to ensure the "irreversibility" of communist control. . . .

Finally, in Cambodia, the worst horror of all: the genocide of at least 1 million Cambodians by the Khmer Rouge, who also took power 10 years ago this month. The Khmer Rouge emptied the cities and murdered the educated; they set out to destroy traditional Cambodian society and to construct a wholly new and "pure" society on the ruins of the old. A French Jesuit who witnessed the early phases of communist rule called it "a perfect example of the application of an ideology pushed to the furthest limit of its internal logic." We say at least 1 million dead. Maybe it was 2 million. The suffering and misery represented by such numbers are beyond our ability to comprehend. Our imaginations are confined by the limits of the civilized life we know.

In December 1978, Vietnam went to war with its erstwhile partners and overthrew the Khmer Rouge regime. Naturally, some Cambodians at first welcomed the Vietnamese as liberators. But as the Vietnamese invaders came to apply in Cambodia the techniques of repression known all too well to the people of Vietnam, resistance in Cambodia grew. . . .

Hanoi's leaders are thus extending their rule to the full boundaries of the former colonial domain, seeking dominion over all of Indochina. Not only do the Vietnamese threaten Thailand—the Soviets, with naval and air bases at Cam Ranh Bay, are now better able to project their power in the Pacific, Southeast Asian, and Indian Ocean regions and to threaten vital Western lines of communication in all these regions. Cam Ranh is now the center of the largest concentration of Soviet naval units outside the U.S.S.R. [Union of Soviet Socialist Republics].

The Moral Issue

What does all this mean? Events since 1975 shed light on the past: this horror was precisely what we were trying to prevent. The President [Ronald Reagan] has called our effort a noble cause, and he was right. Whatever mistakes in how the war was fought, whatever one's view of the strategic rationale for our intervention, the *morality* of our effort must now be clear. Those Americans who served, or who grieve for their loved ones lost or missing, can hold their heads high: our sacrifice was in the service of noble ideals—to save innocent people from brutal tyranny. [U.S. Ambassador to Vietnam] Ellsworth Bunker used to say: no one who dies for freedom ever dies in vain.

We owe all our Vietnam veterans a special debt. They fought with courage and skill under more difficult conditions than Americans in any war before them. They fought with a vague and uncertain mission against a tenacious enemy. They fought knowing that part of the nation opposed their efforts. They suffered abuse when they came home. But like their fathers before them, they fought for what Americans have always fought for: freedom, human dignity, and justice. They are heroes. They honored their country, and we should show them our gratitude.

And when we speak of honor and gratitude, we speak again of our prisoners of war—and of the nearly 2,500 men who remain missing. We will not rest until we have received the fullest possible accounting of the fate of these heroes.

The Strategic Price

We left Indochina in 1975, but the cost of failure was high. The price was paid, in the first instance, by the more than 30 million people we left behind to fall under communist rule. But America, and the world, paid a price.

Our domestic divisions weakened us. The war consumed precious defense resources, and the assault on defense spending at home compounded the cost; years of crucial defense investment were lost, while the Soviets continued the steady military buildup they launched after the Cuban missile crisis. These wasted years are what necessitated our recent defense buildup to restore the global balance.

For a time, the United States retreated into introspection, self-doubt, and hesitancy. Some Americans tended to think that *American* power was the source of the world's problems, and that the key to peace was to limit *our* actions in the world. So we imposed all sorts of restrictions on ourselves. Vietnam—and Watergate—left a legacy of congressional restrictions on presidential flexibility, now embedded in our legislation. Not only the War Powers Resolution but a host of constraints on foreign aid, arms exports, intelligence activities, and other aspects of policy—these weakened the ability of the President to act and to conduct foreign policy, and they weakened our country. Thus we pulled back from global leadership.

Our retreat created a vacuum that was exploited by our adversaries. The Soviets concluded that the global "correlation of forces" was shifting in their favor. They took advantage of our inhibitions and projected their power to unprecedented lengths: intervening in Angola, in Ethiopia, in South Yemen, and in Afghanistan. The Iranian hostage crisis deepened our humiliation.

American weakness turned out to be the most *destabilizing* factor on the global scene. The folly of isolationism was again revealed. Once again it was demonstrated—the hard way—that American engagement, American strength, and American leadership are indispensable to peace. A strong America makes the world a safer place. . . .

The Relevance of the Vietnam Experience

That experience has many other lessons. We acted under many illusions during the Vietnam period, which events since 1975 should have dispelled. We have no excuse for falling prey to the same illusions again.

During the Vietnam war, we heard an endless and shifting sequence of apologies for the communists: that they were "nationalists"; that they were an indigenous anticolonial movement; that they were engaged in a civil war that the outside world should not meddle in. As these arguments were proved hollow, the apologies changed. We heard that a communist victory would not have harmful consequences, either in their countries or the surrounding region. We were told that the communists' ambitions would be satisfied, that their behavior would become moderate. As these assertions became less convincing, the apologies turned to attack those who fought to be free of communism: our friends were denounced as corrupt and dictatorial, unworthy of our support. Their smallest misdeeds were magnified and condemned.

Then we heard the theme that we should not seek "military solutions," that such conflicts were the product of deep-seated economic and social factors. The answer, they said, was not security assistance but aid to develop the economy and raise living standards. But how do you address economic and social needs when communist guerrillas—as in Vietnam then and in Central America now—are waging war *against* the economy in order to maximize hardship? Our economic aid then, as now, is massive; but development must be built on the base of security. And what are the chances for diplomatic solutions if—as we saw after the 1973 Paris agreement—we fail to maintain the balance of strength on which successful negotiation depends? Escapism about the realities of power and security—that is a pretty good definition of isolationism.

And finally, of course, the critics turned their attack on

America. America can do no right, they said. Now, criticism of policy is natural and commonplace in a democracy. But we should bear this past experience in mind in our contemporary debates. The litany of apology for communists, and condemnation for America and our friends, is beginning again. Can we afford to be naive again about the consequences when we pull back, about the special ruthlessness of communist rule? Do the American people really accept the notion that *we,* and our friends, are the representatives of evil?

The American people believe in their country and in its role as a force for good. They want to see an effective foreign policy that blocks aggression and advances the cause of freedom and democracy. They are tired of setbacks, especially those that result from restraints we impose on ourselves. . . .

America's Responsibility

Today, we remember a setback, but the noble cause of defending freedom is still our cause. Our friends and allies still rely on us. Our responsibility remains.

America's Armed Forces are still the bulwark of peace and security for the free world. America's diplomats are still on the front line of efforts to reduce arsenals, settle conflicts, and push back the danger of war.

The larger lesson of the past decade is that when America lost faith in itself, world stability suffered and freedom lost ground. This must never happen again. We carry the banner of liberty, democracy, the dignity of the individual, tolerance, the rule of law. Throughout our history, including the period of Vietnam, we have been the champion of freedom, a haven of opportunity, and a beacon of hope to oppressed peoples everywhere.

Let us be true to the hopes invested in us. Let us live up to our ideals and be their strong and faithful champion around the world.

A Declaration of Interdependence Between the United States and Vietnam

William Jefferson Clinton

During the Vietnam War, William Jefferson Clinton attended Georgetown University, spent two years at Oxford University on a Rhodes scholarship, and earned a law degree at Yale University. At Georgetown University he participated in the antiwar movement and worked as a summer intern for Senator J. William Fulbright, a leader of antiwar sentiment in Congress. While attending Yale, he worked on the presidential campaign of antiwar candidate George McGovern. During Clinton's successful campaign for the 1992 presidential election, political critics highlighted his antiwar activities, questioned the legitimacy of his student draft deferments, and called him a "draft dodger." In the first year of his presidency, he began easing economic sanctions against Vietnam and, on February 3, 1994, he announced the lifting of the trade embargo against Vietnam that the United States had begun soon after American withdrawal from the war. After President Clinton announced the normalization of relations with Vietnam on July 11, 1995, Secretary of State Warren Christopher opened the U.S. embassy in Hanoi on August 5, 1995. Clinton chose Douglas "Pete" Peterson, a former Vietnam War prisoner-of-war in Hanoi, as the first postwar U.S. ambassador to Vietnam, and Peter-

Excerpted from William J. Clinton's remarks at Vietnam National University, November 17, 2000.

son took office in Hanoi on May 9, 1997.

As the first U.S. president to visit Hanoi, President Clinton opens the following address, delivered on November 17, 2000, to students at the Hanoi National University branch of Vietnam National University, by reminding them that Ho Chi Minh's Declaration of Independence for Vietnam quoted Thomas Jefferson's words from the U.S. Declaration of Independence. After reviewing the postwar development of cooperative relations between the United States and Vietnam, he highlights the benefits of globalization and economic interdependence, characterizing a recent bilateral trade agreement as a "declaration of interdependence."

On October 3, 2001, the U.S. Senate approved an agreement normalizing trade relations between the United States and Vietnam, which Vietnam's National Assembly ratified on November 28, 2001, finally ending America's economic war against Vietnam. Thus, a conflict that began in 1945 as an ideological war between the competing economic systems of communism and capitalism, then erupted into a lengthy military conflict that severely stressed the economies of both nations, and became an economic trade war punctuated with cooperative agreements concerning missing soldiers, was finally concluded more than fifty years later with a trade agreement establishing economic interdependence between the people of the United States and Vietnam.

T wo centuries ago, during the early days of the United States, we reached across the seas for partners in trade, and one of the first nations we encountered was Vietnam. In fact, one of our Founding Fathers, Thomas Jefferson, tried to obtain rice seed from Vietnam to grow on his farm in Virginia 200 years ago. By the time World War II arrived, the United States had become a significant consumer of export from Vietnam. In 1945, at the moment of your country's birth, the words of Thomas Jefferson were chosen to be echoed in your own Declaration of Independence: "All men are created equal. The Creator has given us certain inviolable rights—the right to life, the right to be free, the right to achieve happiness."

A Common History

Of course, all of this common history, 200 years of it, has been obscured in the last few decades by the conflict we call the Vietnam war and you call the American war. You may know that in Washington, DC, on our National Mall, there is a stark black granite wall engraved with the name of every single American who died in Vietnam. At this solemn memorial, some American veterans also refer to the "other side of the wall," the staggering sacrifice of the Vietnamese people on both sides of that conflict, more than 3 million brave soldiers and civilians.

This shared suffering has given our countries a relationship unlike any other. Because of the conflict, America is now home to one million Americans of Vietnamese ancestry. Because of the conflict, 3 million American veterans served in Vietnam, as did many journalists, embassy personnel, aid workers, and others who are forever connected to your country.

Almost 20 years ago now, a group of American servicemen took the first step to reestablish contacts between the United States and Vietnam. They traveled back to Vietnam for the first time since the war, and as they walked through the streets of Hanoi, they were approached by Vietnamese citizens who had heard of their visit. "Are you the American soldiers?" they asked. Not sure what to expect, our veterans answered, "Yes, we are." And to their immense relief, their hosts simply said, "Welcome to Vietnam."

More veterans followed, including distinguished American veterans and heroes who serve now in the United States Congress: Senator John McCain, Senator Bob Kerrey, Senator Chuck Robb, and Senator John Kerry from Massachusetts, who is here with me today, along with a number of Representatives from our Congress, some of whom are veterans of the Vietnam conflict.

When they came here, they were determined to honor those who fought, without refighting the battles; to remember our history, but not to perpetuate it; to give young people like you in both our countries the chance to live in your tomorrows, not in our yesterdays. As Ambassador Pete Peterson has said so eloquently, "We cannot change the past. What we can change is the future."

Our New Relationship

Our new relationship gained strength as American veterans launched nonprofit organizations to work on behalf of the Vietnamese people, such as providing devices to people with war injuries to help them lead more normal lives. Vietnam's willingness to help us return the remains of our fallen servicemen to their families has been the biggest boost to improve ties. And there are many Americans here who have worked in that endeavor for many years now, including our Secretary of Veterans Affairs, Hershel Gober.

The desire to be reunited with a lost family member is something we all understand. It touches the hearts of Americans to know that every Sunday in Vietnam, one of your most-watched television shows features families seeking viewers' help in finding loved ones they lost in the war so long ago now. And we are grateful for the Vietnamese villagers who have helped us to find our missing and, therefore, to give their families the peace of mind that comes with knowing what actually happened to their loved ones.

No two nations have ever before done the things we are doing together to find the missing from the Vietnam conflict. Teams of Americans and Vietnamese work together, sometimes in tight and dangerous places. The Vietnamese Government has offered us access to files and Government information to assist our search. And in turn, we have been able to give Vietnam almost 400,000 pages of documents that could assist in your search. On this trip, I have brought with me another 350,000 pages of documents that I hope will help Vietnamese families find out what happened to their missing loved ones.

Today I was honored to present these to your President, Tran Duc Luong. And I told him, before the year is over, America will provide another million pages of documents.

We will continue to offer our help and to ask for your help as we both honor our commitment to do whatever we can for as long as it takes to achieve the fullest possible accounting of our loved ones.

Your cooperation in that mission over these last 8 years has made it possible for America to support international lending to Vietnam, to resume trade between our countries, to establish formal diplomatic relations and, this year, to sign a pivotal trade agreement.

Finally, America is coming to see Vietnam as your people have asked for years, as a country, not a war, a country with the highest literacy rate in Southeast Asia, a country whose young people just won three gold medals at the International Math Olympiad in Seoul, a country of gifted, hard-working entrepreneurs emerging from years of conflict and uncertainty to shape a bright future.

Globalization

Today the United States and Vietnam open a new chapter in our relationship, at a time when people all across the world trade more, travel more, know more about and talk more with each other than ever before. Even as people take pride in their national independence, we know we are becoming more and more interdependent. The movement of people, money, and ideas across borders, frankly, breeds suspicion among many good people in every country. They are worried about globalization because of its unsettling and unpredictable consequences.

Yet, globalization is not something we can hold off or turn off. It is the economic equivalent of a force of nature, like wind or water. We can harness wind to fill a sail. We can use water to generate energy. We can work hard to protect people and property from storms and floods. But there is no point in denying the existence of wind or water, or trying to make them go away. The same is true for globalization. We can work to maximize its benefits and minimize its risks, but we cannot ignore it, and it is not going away.

In the last decade, as the volume of world trade has doubled, investment flows from wealthy nations to developing ones have increased by 6 times, from $25 billion in 1990 to more than $150 billion in 1998. Nations that have opened their economies to the international trading system have grown at least twice as fast as nations with closed economies. Your next job may well depend on foreign trade and investment. Come to think of it, since I have to leave office in about 8 weeks, my next job may depend on foreign trade and investment.

Over the last 15 years, Vietnam launched its policy of Doi Moi [The Doi Moi (literally change and newness) Program was the Vietnamese Communist Party's program for reform and renovation of the economy.], joined APEC [Asia-Pacific Economic Cooperation] and ASEAN [Association of Southeast Asian Nations] normalized relations with the European Union and the United States, and disbanded collective farming, freeing farmers to grow what they want and earn the fruits of their own labor. The results were impressive proof of the power of your markets and the abilities of your people. You not only conquered malnutrition; you became the world's second-largest exporter of rice and achieved stronger overall economic growth.

Of course, in recent years the rate of growth has slowed and foreign investment has declined here, showing that any attempt to remain isolated from the risks of a global economy also guarantees isolation from its rewards, as well.

A Declaration of Interdependence

General Secretary Le Kha Phieu said this summer, and I quote, "We have yet to achieve the level of development commensurate with the possibilities of our country. And there is only one way to further open up the economy." So this summer, in what I believe will be seen as a pivotal step toward your future prosperity, Vietnam joined the United States in signing an historic bilateral trade agreement, building a foundation for Vietnam's entry eventually into the World Trade Organization.

Under the agreement, Vietnam will grant to its citizens, and over time to citizens of other countries, rights to import, export, and distribute goods, giving the Vietnamese people expanding rights to determine their own economic destiny.

Vietnam has agreed it will subject important decisions to the rule of law and the international trading system, increase the flow of information to its people, and accelerate the rise of a free economy and the private sector.

Of course, this will be good for Vietnam's foreign partners, like the United States. But it will be even better for Vietnam's own entrepreneurs, who are working hard to build businesses of their own. Under this agreement, Vietnam could be earning, according to the World Bank, another $1.5 billion each and every year from exports alone.

Both our nations were born with a Declaration of Independence. This trade agreement is a form of declaration of interdependence, a clear, unequivocal statement that prosperity in the 21st century depends upon a nation's economic engagement in the rest of the world.

Engines of Prosperity

This new openness is a great opportunity for you, but it does not guarantee success. What else should be done? Vietnam is such a young country, with 60 percent of your population under the age of 30, and 1.4 million new people entering your work force every year. Your leaders realize that government and state-owned businesses cannot generate 1.4 million new jobs every year. They know that the industries driving the global economy today—computers, telecommunications, biotechnology—these are all based on knowledge. That is why economies all over the world grow faster when young people stay in school longer, when women have the same educational opportunities that men have, when young people like you have every opportunity to explore new ideas and then to turn those ideas into your own business opportunities.

You can be—indeed, those of you in this hall today must be—the engine of Vietnam's future prosperity. As President Tran Duc Luong has said, the internal strength of the country is the intellect and capacity of its people.

The United States has great respect for your intellect and capacity. One of our Government's largest educational exchange programs is with Vietnam, and we want to do more. Senator Kerry is right there, and I mentioned him earlier—is leading an effort in our United States Congress, along with Senator John McCain and other veterans of the conflict here, to establish a new Vietnam Education Foundation. Once enacted, the foundation would support 100 fellowships every year, either here or in the United States, for people to study or teach science, math, technology, and medicine.

We're ready to put more funding in our exchange programs now so this effort can get underway immediately. I hope some of you in this room will have a chance to take part. And I want to thank Senator Kerry for this great idea. Thank you, sir, for what you have done.

American Ideals

Let me say, as important as knowledge is, the benefits of knowledge are necessarily limited by undue restrictions on its use. We Americans believe the freedom to explore, to travel, to think, to speak, to shape decisions that affect our lives enriches the lives of individuals and nations in ways that go far beyond economics.

Now, America's record is not perfect in this area. After all, it took us almost a century to banish slavery. It took us even longer to give women the right to vote. And we are still seeking to live up to the more perfect Union of our Founders' dreams and the words of our Declaration of Independence and Constitution. But along the way over these 226 years— 224 years—we've learned some lessons. For example, we have seen that economies work better where newspapers are free to expose corruption and independent courts can ensure that contracts are honored, that competition is robust and fair, that public officials honor the rule of law.

In our experience, guaranteeing the right to religious worship and the right to political dissent does not threaten the stability of a society. Instead, it builds people's confidence in the fairness of our institutions and enables us to take it when a decision goes in a way we don't agree with. All this makes our country stronger in good times and bad. In our experience, young people are much more likely to have confidence in their future if they have a say in shaping it, in choosing their governmental leaders and having a government that is accountable to those it serves.

Now, let me say emphatically, we do not seek to impose these ideals, nor could we. Vietnam is an ancient and enduring country. You have proved to the world that you will make your own decisions. Only you can decide, for example, if you will continue to share Vietnam's talents and ideas with the world, if you will continue to open Vietnam so that you can enrich it with the insights of others. Only you can decide if you will continue to open your markets, open your society, and strengthen the rule of law. Only you can decide how to weave individual liberties and human rights into the rich and strong fabric of Vietnamese national identity.

Your future should be in your hands, the hands of the Vietnam people. But your future is important to the rest of us, as well. For as Vietnam succeeds, it will benefit this region and your trading partners and your friends throughout the world.

We are eager to increase our cooperation with you across the board. We want to continue our work to clear landmines and unexploded ordnance. We want to strengthen our common efforts to protect the environment by phasing out leaded gasoline in Vietnam, maintaining a clean water supply, saving coral reefs and tropical forests. We want to bolster our efforts on disaster relief and prevention, including our efforts to help those suffering from the floods in the Mekong Delta. Yesterday we presented to your Government satellite imagery from our Global Disaster Information Network, images that show in great detail the latest flood levels on the Delta, that can help Vietnam to rebuild.

We want to accelerate our cooperation in science, cooperation focused this month on our meeting in Singapore to study together the health and ecological effects of dioxin [a toxic chemical found in defoliants used during the Vietnam War] on the people of Vietnam and the Americans who were in Vietnam, and cooperation that we are advancing further with the science and technology agreement our two countries signed just today.

We want to be your ally in the fight against killer diseases like AIDS, tuberculosis, and malaria. I am glad to announce that we will nearly double our support of Vietnam's efforts to contain the AIDS crisis through education, prevention, care, and treatment. We want to work with you to make Vietnam a safer place by giving you help to reduce preventable injuries on the streets, at home, and in the workplace. We want to work with you to make the most of this trade agreement by providing technical assistance to assure its full and smooth implementation, and finding ways to encourage greater United States investment in your country.

We are, in short, eager to build our partnership with Vietnam. We believe it's good for both our nations.

We believe the Vietnamese people have the talent to succeed in this new global age, as they have in the past. We know it because we've seen the progress you have made in this last decade. We have seen the talent and ingenuity of the Vietnamese who have come to settle in America. Vietnamese-Americans have become elected officials, judges, leaders in science and in our high-tech industry. . . .

Vietnamese-Americans have flourished not just because of their unique abilities and their good values but also because they have had the opportunity to make the most of their abilities and their values. As your opportunities grow, to live, to learn, to express your creativity, there will be no stopping the people of Vietnam. And you will find, I am certain, that the American people will be by your side. For in this interdependent world, we truly do have a stake in your success.

Almost 200 years ago, at the beginning of the relations between the United States and Vietnam, our two nations made many attempts to negotiate a treaty of commerce, sort of like the trade agreement that we signed today. But 200 years ago, they all failed, and no treaty was concluded. Listen to what one historian said about what happened 200 years ago, and think how many times it could have been said in the two centuries since. He said, "These efforts failed because two distant cultures were talking past each other, and the importance of each to the other was insufficient to overcome these barriers."

Let the days when we talk past each other be gone for good. Let us acknowledge our importance to one another. Let us continue to help each other heal the wounds of war, not by forgetting the bravery shown and the tragedy suffered by all sides but by embracing the spirit of reconciliation and the courage to build better tomorrows for our children.

May our children learn from us that good people, through respectful dialog, can discover and rediscover their common humanity and that a painful, painful past can be redeemed in a peaceful and prosperous future.

Appendix of Biographies

George Wildman Ball

During the Vietnam War, George Wildman Ball served as under-secretary of state for the Kennedy and Johnson administrations, wrote extensively on foreign affairs, formulated U.S. foreign aid and foreign trade policies, and promoted strong ties between the United States and Europe. His role during the Vietnam War became widely known with the publication of the Pentagon Papers in 1971. Alone among foreign policy advisers of Presidents Kennedy and Johnson, he consistently questioned American involvement in Vietnam and argued that intervention would not succeed. His views were partly based on his conviction that Southeast Asia mattered less to the United States in the struggle against communism than did the industrial powers of Europe, the Middle East, and Japan.

Ball was born in Des Moines, Iowa, on December 21, 1909. After receiving his law degree from Northwestern University, Ball went to Washington, D.C., in 1933 to work for the Farm Credit Administration and then for the Department of Treasury. In 1935 he returned to Chicago to practice law in two firms, one of which included Adlai E. Stevenson. From 1942 to 1944 he worked in the Office of Lend-Lease Administration and in the Foreign Economic Administration. In 1944 he was appointed director of the U.S. Strategic Bombing Survey in London. Ball returned to Washington in 1945 to become general counsel for the French Supply Council, working toward the creation of the European Coal and Steel Community and the European Common Market.

During the 1950s Ball supported the presidential campaigns of Adlai Stevenson, managing the candidate's 1960 campaign at the Los Angeles convention. John F. Kennedy won the nomination and the election, naming Ball as undersecretary of state for economic affairs in January 1961.

Serving under Secretary of State Dean Rusk in the Kennedy and Johnson administrations, Ball concentrated on trade matters, helping to draft the Trade Expansion Act of 1962. Rusk, with whom Ball became close friends, gave Ball free rein in the State Department and in expressing his views to the president about Vietnam and other controversial issues.

In September 1966 Ball resigned, returning to government briefly when President Johnson appointed him ambassador to the

United Nations in 1968. He resigned that post to help Hubert Humphrey's presidential campaign. In private life, Ball became an investment banker with Lehman Brothers and wrote regularly on foreign affairs, frequently criticizing the administrations of the 1970s and 1980s, until his death on May 26, 1994.

William Jefferson Clinton

William Jefferson "Bill" Clinton was born in Hope, Arkansas, on August 19, 1946, and named William Jefferson Blyth IV after his father, who had been killed before his birth. After his mother's marriage to Roger Clinton, Bill changed his last name to Clinton. In 1963, as an American Legion Boys' Nation delegate, he met President John F. Kennedy and decided that he wanted a career in politics.

As a college student at Georgetown University during the Vietnam War, Clinton was committed to the antiwar movement. He graduated from Georgetown in 1968 and spent the next two years at Oxford University on a Rhodes scholarship. While attending law school at Yale, Clinton became a campaign coordinator for an antiwar senatorial candidate and for presidential candidate George McGovern.

After school, Clinton practiced law in Arkansas and taught at the University of Arkansas. In 1976 he won election as attorney general for Arkansas, an office he held from 1977 to 1979. In 1978 Clinton ran for governor of Arkansas and won, becoming the youngest governor in Arkansas history. In November 1980 Clinton lost his bid for reelection but was reelected in 1982, serving as governor until 1992.

Clinton was elected president in November 1992, defeating Republican incumbent George Bush and third-party candidate Ross Perot. In 1996 Clinton was reelected, winning by a landslide. However, in 1998, as a result of indiscretions with a White House intern, the House of Representatives impeached him, although the Senate acquitted Clinton of the charges.

As president, Clinton addressed economic issues, especially international trade agreements. His administration passed the North American Free Trade Agreement that made a single trading bloc of the United States, Canada, and Mexico, and it normalized trade relations with China and Vietnam. As the first U.S. president to address Russia's parliament, on June 5, 2000, he urged Russia's legislators to continue strengthening democracy and the nation's economy. In the process of normalizing relations with Vietnam, Clinton became the first American president to visit a unified Vietnam on November 13, 2000.

John Foster Dulles

John Foster Dulles was born in Washington, D.C., on February 25, 1888. After graduating from Princeton and the law school of George Washington University, Dulles joined the international law firm of Sullivan and Cromwell in 1911, becoming a partner in 1920 and head of the firm in 1927.

He attended the 1919 Paris Peace Conference as legal counsel to the American delegation and, as legal adviser to the U.S. delegation in 1945, he helped draw up the charter of the United Nations. After serving in a vacated seat in the U.S. Senate from 1949 to 1950, Dulles became ambassador-at-large for President Harry S. Truman and negotiated a peace treaty with Japan in 1951. In 1952 Dulles, whose grandfather had been secretary of state for Benjamin Harrison and whose uncle had been secretary of state for Woodrow Wilson, became secretary of state for Dwight D. Eisenhower. In that position, he became the chief architect of the U.S. Cold War policy for containing communism.

During his first months in office, Dulles negotiated an armistice in the Korean War. In Europe, he supported the North Atlantic Treaty Organization. In the Far East, he negotiated the formation of the Southeast Asia Treaty Organization, an eight-nation alliance that was an important element of the U.S. strategy to contain communism in Southeast Asia and especially in Vietnam. In the Middle East, he organized a similar organization, the Central Treaty Organization, and he helped negotiate the United States through the Suez Canal crisis of 1956. Against the Soviet Union, Dulles authored the hard-line policy of brinkmanship, which dared an opponent to approach the brink of nuclear destruction before negotiating a settlement.

Suffering from cancer, Dulles, a dedicated public servant, continued as secretary of state until a month before his death on May 24, 1959.

James William Fulbright

James William Fulbright was born on April 9, 1905, in Sumner, Missouri. After graduating from the University of Arkansas in 1925, he attended Oxford University as a Rhodes scholar. After receiving his law degree from George Washington University in 1934, he worked in the Department of Justice and taught at George Washington University and at the University of Arkansas. From 1939 to 1941, Fulbright was president of the University of Arkansas, the youngest university president in the country.

Fulbright won election to the U.S. House of Representatives in 1942 and became a member of the Foreign Affairs Committee. In September 1943 the House adopted the Fulbright Resolution, supporting international peacekeeping machinery and encouraging U.S participation in what would become the United Nations. In 1945 Fulbright entered the Senate, and his legislation in 1946 establishing the Fulbright Program for international educational exchange passed without debate. In a career marked by dissent, he was the only senator to vote against an appropriation for Senator Joseph McCarthy's investigations in 1956, and he voiced his objection to President Kennedy's planned Bay of Pigs invasion in 1961.

In 1949 Fulbright joined the Senate Foreign Relations Committee, and from 1959 to 1974 he served as chairman, becoming a leading critic of U.S. foreign policy and of U.S. involvement in the Vietnam War. Although Fulbright, a personal friend of President Lyndon B. Johnson, had supported the 1964 Gulf of Tonkin Resolution giving Johnson authorization to use "all necessary steps, including the use of armed force" in Southeast Asia, he became convinced that American fears of communism were becoming an antirevolutionary posture, and he began a campaign to withdraw that authority and to curb Johnson's foreign interventions. Beginning in 1966, Fulbright's committee held widely publicized hearings on U.S. involvement in Vietnam, and Congress eventually denied the president's right to send American forces into hostilities without congressional approval. Fulbright won his fifth term as senator in 1968 but was defeated in 1974.

After leaving the Senate, he worked in a Washington law firm. In 1993 Fulbright received the Presidential Medal of Freedom from President Bill Clinton, who had been his intern during the 1960s. When Fulbright died on February 9, 1995, the Fulbright Program had awarded more than 250,000 scholarships bearing his name and contributing to the goal "to assist in the development of friendly, sympathetic, and peaceful relations between the United States and other countries of the world."

Barry Morris Goldwater

Barry Morris Goldwater was born in Phoenix, Arizona, on January 1, 1909. After graduating from Staunton Military Academy in Virginia, he completed one year at the University of Arizona before dropping out to join the family department store business when his father died in 1929. During World War II he served in the U.S. Army Air Force as a pilot on supply runs. He began his political career in 1949 by winning a Phoenix city council seat. In 1952 he won a Senate seat by campaigning as a staunchly conservative critic of "Trumanism." He supported Senator Joseph McCarthy's campaign against communism and was one of only twenty-two Republican senators who voted against censuring McCarthy in December 1954.

Reelected in 1958, Goldwater enhanced his image as the leader of extreme conservatism by publishing his book *The Conscience of the Conservative*, which sold 3.5 million copies. In 1964 he won the Republican Party's nomination for president by defeating Nelson Rockefeller's moderate Republicans. The famous statement in his acceptance speech that "extremism in the defense of liberty is no vice" enhanced public perception of Goldwater as a dangerous extremist. Lyndon Johnson won in a landslide.

In 1968, as Richard Nixon won the presidency, Goldwater won reelection to the Senate, where he backed American military involvement in Vietnam and supported Nixon's aggressive policies. Goldwater won reelection in 1974, and when President Gerald Ford's defeat in 1976 put Jimmy Carter in the White House, Goldwater opposed Carter on nearly every issue. In 1980 Goldwater won a fifth Senate term, and his support for Ronald Reagan, who had campaigned for him in 1964, helped Reagan easily defeat Carter, although Goldwater spoke against the Reagan Moral Majority's desire to use government to influence morality.

After his retirement in 1987, Goldwater continued to influence American politics with his writing and speeches. In 1996 he suffered a stroke and Alzheimer's disease began to appear; Goldwater died on May 29, 1998.

Ho Chi Minh

Ho Chi Minh was born Nguyen That Thanh on May 19, 1890, in central Vietnam. At age seventeen, he received a minor degree and taught elementary school. In 1911 Ho left Vietnam as a cook on a French ship. He lived in New York, London, and Paris, working odd jobs and publishing criticisms of French colonialism. Ho, whose primary interest was Vietnamese independence, joined the French Socialist Party; when the party split on the colonial issue, Ho joined the founders of the French Communist Party.

Beginning in 1923, Ho studied communism in the Soviet Union and in China. In February 1930 Ho founded the Indochinese Communist Party in opposition to French colonialism. After Japanese forces occupied Vietnam during World War II, Ho returned to his homeland in February 1941 and founded the League for Vietnamese Independence, called the Vietminh, to coordinate the struggle for independence. At this time, he adopted the name Ho Chi Minh, meaning "He Who Enlightens." During the war Ho collaborated with both the Chinese and the Americans in gathering intelligence against the Japanese in exchange for assistance.

Following Japan's surrender, the Vietminh overthrew the puppet regime of Emperor Bao Dai, and on September 2, 1945, Ho proclaimed Vietnam's independence. Ho had unsuccessfully sought Allied recognition against the French, so when war began with the French in December 1946, Ho sought and eventually received weapons and advice from the Chinese. In July 1954 Vietminh forces defeated French forces at Dien Bien Phu, ending the first Vietnam War. A peace agreement, signed in Geneva in July 1954, partitioned Vietnam along the seventeenth parallel and provided for a general election to be held within two years to reunify the country. When the election never happened, Ho ordered the resumption of guerrilla activities in South Vietnam. The United States responded with increased military assistance, sent combat troops into South Vietnam, and began a systematic bombing of North Vietnam.

For several years Ho refused U.S. offers to negotiate a peace settlement, hoping that American public opinion would force the United States to sue for peace. In 1968 he finally agreed to send his representatives to peace talks with Lyndon Johnson's representatives in Paris, where negotiations continued without progress into Richard Nixon's administration. In August 1969 Nixon requested secret negotiations and Ho agreed, but several days later Ho Chi Minh died on September 3, 1969.

Lyndon Baines Johnson

Lyndon Baines Johnson was born on August 27, 1908, near Johnson City, Texas. He graduated from Southwest State Teachers College and taught high school until 1931, when he went to Washington, D.C., as secretary to a Texas congressman. In 1937 Johnson won election to the House of Representatives. In 1948 he won a Senate seat. In 1953 he became the youngest minority leader and, in 1954, the youngest majority leader in Senate history. In 1960, as John F. Kennedy's running mate, Johnson became vice president, and when Kennedy was assassinated on November 22, 1963, Johnson became president.

As president, Johnson created one of the most extensive legislative programs in history, including aid to education and health, children's vaccinations, Medicare, Medicaid, urban renewal, beautification, conservation, development of depressed regions, housing and community development, a war against poverty, control and prevention of crime, civil rights, removing obstacles to the right to vote, and space exploration. Nevertheless, two issues haunted—and eventually ended—his presidency: rioting in black ghettos and the Vietnam War.

When Johnson became president, sixteen thousand American troops were in Vietnam as military advisers; Johnson increased that number to twenty-seven thousand within a few months. Using the authority given to him by the 1964 Gulf of Tonkin Resolution, he began sustained bombing of North Vietnam in early 1965 and landed troops in South Vietnam in March 1965.

Beginning with his speech at Johns Hopkins University in April 1965, in which he offered American aid in reconstruction of Vietnam, Johnson attempted to invite peace talks, but the lack of response from the North Vietnamese led him to continue escalating the war. By 1968 the costs of the Vietnam War were undermining Johnson's Great Society program and his war policies were under attack by Congress and by the American people. On March 31, 1968, President Johnson startled the nation and the world by limiting the bombing of North Vietnam and withdrawing as a candidate for reelection so that he could seek peace in Southeast Asia unimpeded by politics. In April 1968 North Vietnam agreed to participate in peace talks. Negotiations began in Paris in May and, on October 31, 1968, Johnson ended the bombing of North Vietnam that he had begun in 1965. Johnson retired to his ranch in Texas, where he suffered a heart attack and died on January 22, 1973, the day before President Richard Nixon announced the peace treaty that would end the Vietnam War.

John Fitzgerald Kennedy

John Fitzgerald Kennedy was born in Brookline, Massachusetts, on May 29, 1917. After graduating from Harvard University in 1940, he entered the navy. As a PT boat commander during World War II, he became a hero by rescuing his injured crewman after his boat was destroyed. In 1946 he won election to the House of Representatives and reelection in 1948 and in 1950. As a congressman, Kennedy supported President Harry S. Truman's social welfare programs, but he opposed Truman's foreign policies, especially American intervention in Korea. In 1952 Kennedy won a seat in the Senate, which he won again in 1958. With Lyndon Johnson as his running mate, Kennedy won the presidency in 1960 by narrowly defeating Richard Nixon, becoming the youngest president in U.S. history.

Profiles in Courage, Kennedy's biographical profiles of Americans who exercised moral courage at crisis points in their lives, became a best-seller in 1956 and won the Pulitzer Prize for biography in 1957. The Kennedy administration was also characterized by a series of crises. With his civil rights bills stalled in Congress, the president and his brother, Attorney General Robert F. Kennedy, sent federal marshals to southern states to protect Freedom Riders and African American students. In the Bay of Pigs fiasco of April 1961, exiled Cubans invaded Cuba in an unsuccessful American-supported attempt to overthrow Fidel Castro. During the Berlin crisis of August 1961, East Germans erected a wall of concrete blocks between East Berlin and West Berlin while Kennedy asserted that the United States would not abandon West Berlin. During the Cuban Missile Crisis of October 1962, Kennedy told the nation that the Soviet Union had deployed nuclear missiles in Cuba and declared that the United States would not allow Cuba to become a Soviet missile base. After seven days of tense brinkmanship with Soviet premier Nikita Khrushchev, the Soviets removed the missiles and eventually signed a nuclear treaty with the United States.

President John F. Kennedy was the first president to face nuclear confrontation, the first to reach for the moon with the American space programs, and the first to put the power of the presidency behind civil rights. Yet most of his legislative programs for tax reform, civil rights, and Medicare stalled in Congress. In addition, despite his original opposition, he escalated American involvement in South Vietnam by supporting the corrupt Ngo Dinh Diem regime with financial aid, by increasing the number of U.S. military advisers from nine hundred to sixteen thousand, and by supporting the military coup that overthrew and assassinated Diem on November 1, 1963. Kennedy was assassinated by Lee Harvey Oswald in Dallas, Texas, on November 22, 1963.

Robert Francis Kennedy

Robert Francis Kennedy was born on November 20, 1925, in Brookline, Massachusetts. He left Harvard University to join the navy during World War II, but he returned in 1946. After graduating from Harvard in 1948, he earned his law degree from the University of Virginia. In 1951 Kennedy joined the criminal division of the U.S. Department of Justice, but he resigned the following year to run his brother John F. Kennedy's successful campaign for the Senate. In 1953 Kennedy became assistant counsel to Senator Joseph McCarthy's Senate subcommittee on investigations, but he resigned later that year in protest against McCarthy's methods. From 1955 to 1960, Kennedy served as counsel to several Senate committees and gained national fame while investigating teamsters-union leader James Hoffa.

In 1960 Robert Kennedy managed John F. Kennedy's successful presidential campaign and subsequently became attorney general in John's administration, helping his brother with the Berlin crisis, the Cuban Missile Crisis, civil rights crises, and the escalating war in Vietnam.

Soon after President Kennedy's assassination in 1963, Robert Kennedy resigned from Lyndon Johnson's administration to run successfully for senator in 1964. As a senator, Kennedy took special interest in social welfare and civil rights issues, and he reversed his prior stance on Vietnam, calling for deescalation of American involvement. In 1968 Kennedy began his run for the presidency. Drawing support from African Americans, young people, antiwar activists, and blue-collar workers, he won primaries in Indiana, Nebraska, South Dakota, and California. On the night of June 4, 1968, following a narrow victory in the California primaries, Kennedy was shot by Sirhan B. Sirhan; he died on June 6, 1968.

John Forbes Kerry

John Forbes Kerry was born on December 22, 1943, in Denver, Colorado. In 1966, after denouncing the Vietnam War in his commencement speech at Yale, Kerry enlisted in the U.S. Navy and served as a gunboat officer on the Mekong Delta in Vietnam. After winning the Silver Star, the Bronze Star, and three Purple Hearts for his heroism, Kerry obtained an early release from the navy and became a leader of Vietnam Veterans Against the War (VVAW) and a cofounder of the Vietnam Veterans of America. As a VVAW leader, Kerry organized numerous demonstrations against the war and testified about the war before the Senate Foreign Relations Committee.

After earning a law degree from Boston College in 1976, he worked as an assistant district attorney, taught college classes, and opened a law practice. In 1982 he won the race for lieutenant governor of Massachusetts. In 1984 he won a Senate seat. From 1986 until 1989, Kerry led a Senate investigation into the Reagan administration's Iran-contra drugs-for-arms affair. He discovered Oliver North's involvement, that the United States had known that Panamanian dictator Manuel Noriega was a drug lord, and that the Bank of Credit and Commerce International served as a drug-money launderer for the CIA. During his second term as senator, from 1990 until 1996, Kerry pushed the government to declassify records regarding soldiers missing during the Vietnam War.

Currently in his third Senate term, Kerry has championed environmental issues, public education reform, international trade agreements, children's issues, a balanced budget, reduction of corporate welfare, and campaign finance reform. In November 2000 Kerry accompanied President Bill Clinton to Hanoi to normalize relations with Vietnam.

Martin Luther King Jr.

Martin Luther King Jr. was born on January 15, 1929, in Atlanta, Georgia. King entered Morehouse College at the age of fifteen and graduated in 1948. After being ordained at the age of nineteen, King graduated from Crozer Theological Seminary in 1951 and received his doctorate in theology from Boston University in 1955.

King's civil rights activities began in 1955, after Rosa Parks, a black woman, was arrested for violating a segregated seating ordinance on a public bus in Montgomery, Alabama. King and fellow minister Ralph Abernathy formed the Montgomery Improvement Association to boycott the bus company. The bus company capitulated, the U.S. Supreme Court affirmed that the bus segregation laws were unconstitutional, and King became a national hero and a leader in the civil rights struggle. After that victory, King's life was in constant danger. His home was bombed, he was frequently threatened, and he was arrested thirty times for civil rights activities.

In January 1957 King became president of the Southern Christian Leadership Conference (SCLC), a civil rights organization composed of black ministers, which King would lead until his death in 1968. Under King's leadership, the SCLC sponsored nonviolent civil rights activities nationwide to double the number of black voters in the South, to end segregation at lunch counters in city stores, to end segregated public transportation, and to gain fair employment for African Americans. On August 27, 1963, over 250,000 citizens assembled in Washington, D.C., for a mass civil rights rally in which King delivered his famous "Let Freedom Ring" address. A few weeks later President Lyndon B. Johnson signed the 1964 Civil Rights Bill. King received the Nobel Peace Prize for his nonviolent activities in December 1964. In 1965 King encouraged President Johnson to expedite passage of the Voting Rights Bill by marching from Selma to Montgomery to demonstrate African American determination to vote.

By 1967 King had become troubled by American involvement in the Vietnam War and began speaking against the war at antiwar demonstrations. In January 1968 King and other antiwar leaders called for a Washington rally in February. He also announced that the Poor People's March would converge in Washington on April

22. In Memphis on April 3, King addressed a rally and, speaking of threats on his life, he urged followers to continue the nonviolent struggle no matter what happened to him. On April 4, 1968, as King stood on an outside balcony at the Lorraine Hotel, he was shot by James Earl Ray and he died that evening.

Le Duan

Le Duan, whose birth name is not known, was born April 7, 1908, in central Vietnam. After receiving a French colonial education, he worked as a clerk for the Vietnam Railway Company. Threatened with arrest by French authorities for political activities, Le Duan fled the country when he was eighteen years old.

In 1930 Le Duan became a founding member of the Indochinese Communist Party. After returning to Vietnam, Le Duan was convicted of "conspiracy against national security" and was imprisoned at the Poulo Condore Prison from 1931 until 1936, when he was released under a French political amnesty program. In 1940, after the outbreak of World War II, the French colonialists returned Le Duan to Poulo Condore Prison, where he stayed until the departing Japanese released him at the end of the war.

After joining Ho Chi Minh's Vietminh in defeating the French, he successfully increased postwar agricultural production by collectivizing farms. Le Duan became party secretary-general, with Ho as party chairman, at the Third Party Congress in 1960. During the Vietnam War, Le Duan developed strategies of guerrilla warfare for the National Liberation Front (Vietcong) in South Vietnam against South Vietnamese and American forces. After the war, Le Duan led the disastrous economic restructure of Vietnam, proving to be much less successful as a peacetime leader. He was reportedly treated several times in Moscow for a liver ailment during the 1980s, and the Voice of Vietnam radio announced his death on July 10, 1986.

Wayne Lyman Morse

Wayne Lyman Morse was born on a Wisconsin farm on October 20, 1900. He attended the University of Wisconsin, the University of Minnesota, and Columbia University, receiving his law degree from Columbia. By the age of thirty-one, Morse was a full professor and the dean of the University of Oregon's School of Law. Morse developed a national reputation as a labor arbitrator and was appointed by President Franklin Roosevelt to the National War Labor Board during World War II.

Morse won a seat in the Senate on the Republican ticket in 1944 and won again in 1950. As a liberal Republican, Morse opposed his party's Taft-Hartley Labor Act of 1947 and opposed its presidential nominee in 1952, Dwight Eisenhower, due to Eisenhower's choice of Senator Richard Nixon as his running mate. After Eisenhower defeated Adlai Stevenson, Morse dropped his Republican Party allegiance and served his second Senate term as an Independent. In 1956, running as a Progressive Democrat, Morse won his third term, and he won again in 1962. As a senator, Morse championed civil rights, labor rights, and social reform, and he opposed the death penalty and corporate domination of the political process.

In August 1964 Congress approved the Gulf of Tonkin Resolution, granting authority to President B. Lyndon Johnson to use "all necessary steps, including the use of armed force" to defend South Vietnam. Morse joined Senator Ernest Gruening in opposing the measure against the 502 congressmen who voted for it. Morse opposed the resolution on constitutional grounds, declaring that Congress was surrendering its constitutional authority. Throughout the remainder of his term, Morse protested Johnson's deceptive conduct of the Vietnam War, paying the political price for his protest when he lost his reelection bid in 1968. Morse ran again unsuccessfully in 1972. In 1974 he won the Democratic senatorial nomination, but he died while campaigning on July 22, 1974.

Richard Milhous Nixon

Richard Milhous Nixon was born on his father's lemon farm in Yorba Linda, California, on January 9, 1913. Graduating from Whittier College, he received his law degree at Duke University and practiced law in Whittier, California. Before World War II, Nixon worked in the Office of Emergency Management until 1942, when he entered the navy to serve as an operations officer and as a naval lawyer. In September 1945, asked by Whittier Republicans to run for Congress, he mustered out of the navy to begin his victorious campaign.

As congressman, Nixon became a leading anti-Communist member of the House Un-American Activities Committee. His conviction of Alger Hiss, a former State Department official charged with Communist connections, brought Nixon national fame. In 1950 he won a Senate seat and served two years before becoming Dwight Eisenhower's running mate in the 1952 presidential election. During the campaign, Nixon was charged with having received illegal funds collected from private citizens. He responded with a televised defense that saved his candidacy and helped Eisenhower win the presidency.

As the Republican presidential candidate in 1960, Nixon lost by a narrow margin to John F. Kennedy and returned to California to practice law. After losing the California gubernatorial election in 1962, he worked for a New York law firm until 1968, when he again became the Republican candidate for president. Running against Vice President Hubert Humphrey and third-party candidate George Wallace, he campaigned on a "secret plan" to end the Vietnam War and won.

As president, he began withdrawing American troops from Vietnam while negotiating with North Vietnam at the Paris peace talks. On an Asian tour in July 1969, he announced the "Nixon Doctrine," which stated that the United States would honor its treaty commitments but would not bear the brunt of fighting in another country. In a televised address to the nation in November 1969, Nixon explained his secret plan, called "Vietnamization," to reduce American presence in Vietnam while shifting defense responsibilities to the South Vietnamese forces. He also began a campaign to neutralize antiwar sentiment and the growing influence of the antiwar movement. Meanwhile, adopting Henry Kissinger's strategy of negotiating from a position of strength, Nixon escalated the war by bombing North Vietnamese sanctuaries in Cambodia, by sending American troops into Cambodia, by bombing North Vietnam, and by mining North Vietnamese harbors. In 1972 Nixon visited China and the Soviet Union, easing relationships with those North Vietnamese allies. In January 1973 Kissinger and North Vietnamese negotiator Le Duc Tho reached a cease-fire agreement, ending the Vietnam War.

During the presidential election of 1972, Nixon had won reelection against George McGovern in a landslide, but a break-in at Democratic national headquarters in the Watergate apartment complex had been traced to Nixon's reelection committee. Nixon denied any personal involvement in the Watergate scandal, but the Supreme Court forced him to release tape recordings that indicated that he had obstructed the FBI investigation. Nixon became the first U.S. president to resign on August 8, 1973. Gerald Ford, whom Nixon had appointed as vice president when Spiro Agnew had resigned to face charges of bribery and income tax evasion in 1973, became president. One month later President Ford pardoned Nixon for any crimes he might have committed as president.

As a private citizen, Nixon became an elder statesman, visiting foreign countries, consulting with the Bush and Clinton administrations, and writing books on foreign affairs until he died on April 22, 1994.

Carl Oglesby

Carl Oglesby was born in Akron, Ohio, in 1935. He dropped out of Kent State University to work as an actor and a playwright in New York City and as a technical editor for Goodyear Aerospace Company. In 1958 he enrolled at the University of Michigan, where he graduated and took an editing job at Bendix Aviation.

After members of the Students for a Democratic Society (SDS) read Oglesby's paper comparing U.S. policy in China with U.S. policy in Vietnam, several of them met with him and invited his participation. In the spring of 1965 Oglesby joined the SDS, participating in the first teach-in at the University of Michigan, in a draft demonstration in New York, and in the march on Washington, D.C., in April 1965. At a convention later that year, Oglesby became president of SDS, a position he would hold for the next three years as he traveled around the country speaking against the war.

Currently, Oglesby is a political writer and the author of many books and articles.

Ronald Wilson Reagan

Born on February 6, 1911, in Tampico, Illinois, Ronald Wilson Reagan, nicknamed "Dutch," attended Eureka College and, after graduating in 1932, worked as a radio sports announcer. In 1937 Reagan took a screen test with Warner Brothers, beginning an acting career that included more than fifty films. During World War II Reagan made training films for the U.S. Army Air Corps; after his discharge in December 1945, he resumed his film career. As president of the Screen Actors Guild, Reagan became an anti-Communist political activist, cooperating with Senator Joseph McCarthy's House Un-American Activities Committee investigations of Hollywood and speaking against communism nationwide.

In October 1964 Reagan received national attention with a televised speech in support of Barry Goldwater's presidential campaign. In 1965 Republicans recruited Reagan to run in the 1966 election for governor of California, which he won. As governor, Reagan sent state troopers to quell campus antiwar protests several times and reduced state funding for universities where protests were tolerated.

In 1970 Reagan won reelection to the California governorship. Although he lost the presidential nomination to Gerald Ford in 1976, he became the Republican frontrunner for the 1980 nomination after Jimmy Carter defeated Ford during the 1976 election. In 1980 Reagan won the presidency over Carter and won reelection over Walter Mondale in 1984.

During his eight years, President Reagan implemented an economic plan that increased defense spending, reduced taxes, and reduced domestic spending, leading to record-high budget deficits. Toward the end of his presidency, Iran-contra investigations revealed that Reagan's administration had secretly sold arms to Iran and had diverted some of the profits to the Nicaraguan anti-Communist "contras." Reagan's claim to have been uninformed only raised questions about his leadership.

After leaving office, Reagan announced in 1994 that he had been diagnosed with Alzheimer's disease and, as his condition deteriorated, he withdrew from public appearances.

David Dean Rusk

On February 9, 1909, David Dean Rusk was born in Cherokee County, Georgia. Graduating from Davidson College in 1931, Rusk attended Oxford for three years on a Rhodes scholarship. From 1934 to 1940, he taught at Mills College, becoming dean of faculty in 1938. During World War II he served in army intelligence, and after his 1946 discharge he joined the State Department, moved to the War Department, then returned to the State Department in 1947 as successor to Alger Hiss in the Office of Special Political Affairs.

Rusk worked in the State Department for the next five years, becoming assistant secretary of state and playing a significant role in Korean War decisions during the Truman administration. In 1952 he left the State Department to become president of the Rockefeller Foundation. In 1960 President John F. Kennedy chose Rusk to be secretary of state, a post he would hold under Kennedy and President Johnson from January 21, 1961, to January 20, 1969. Rusk's policy was to express his dissent with the president in private and to support the president's decisions in public. Rusk opposed the Bay of Pigs invasion, opposed an air strike against Russian offensive weapons during the Cuban Missile Crisis in favor of the naval quarantine ultimately adopted, opposed Kennedy's introduction of ground troops to South Vietnam in 1961, disapproved of the regime of South Vietnamese president Ngo Dinh Diem, and opposed Johnson's escalation of American involvement and his bombing of North Vietnam. Nevertheless, Rusk publicly defended the conduct of the Vietnam War until he left office. Upon leaving office, Rusk taught at the University of Georgia until his death on December 21, 1994.

George Pratt Shultz

George Pratt Shultz, who served five U.S. presidents, was the first director of the Office of Management and Budget and served as secretary of the Department of Labor, the Department of the Treasury, and the State Department.

Shultz was born in New York City on December 13, 1920. After graduating from Princeton University in 1942, he joined the Marine Corps during World War II. Shultz earned his doctorate degree from the Massachusetts Institute of Technology in 1949 and taught there until 1957, also serving on President Dwight D. Eisenhower's Council of Economic Advisors during this time. In 1957 Shultz joined the University of Chicago Graduate School of Business, becoming dean in 1962. Presidents John F. Kennedy and Lyndon B. Johnson appointed Schultz to several government task forces and committees related to labor-management and employment policies.

On December 11, 1968, President Richard M. Nixon named Shultz secretary of labor. After eighteen months, he accepted Nixon's appointment as the first director of the Office of Management and Budget. In May 1972 Nixon named Shultz secretary of the treasury, a position he held until March 1974, when he resigned to join Bechtel Corporation. On July 16, 1982, Shultz became the secretary of state under President Ronald Reagan, serving from 1982 to 1989, at which time he joined Stanford University's Hoover Institute and Graduate School of Business.

Harry S. Truman

Harry S. Truman was born in Lamar, Missouri, on May 8, 1884. After high school he farmed his parents' land until 1917, when he enlisted in the artillery during World War I. Truman began his political career as a judge from 1922 to 1934. He won election to the Senate in 1934 and reelection in 1940. When Franklin Roosevelt was nominated for a fourth presidential term in June 1944, he chose Truman as his running mate. After eighty-two days as vice president, Truman became president when Roosevelt died suddenly on April 12, 1945. A few months into his term, he authorized the dropping of atomic bombs on Japan in August 1945 and subsequently approved the surrender of the Japanese in a treaty signed on September 2, 1945, ending World War II.

While Truman struggled with postwar economic problems in the United States, the State Department under Secretary of State Dean Acheson became alarmed at the spread of communism through Eastern Europe. When Turkey and Greece seemed on the threshold of defeat by Communist elements, Truman delivered an address to Congress on March 2, 1947, in which he announced the Truman Doctrine, declaring that the United States would support all free peoples who were resisting attempted subjugation either by armed minorities at home or aggressors outside their borders.

During Truman's second presidential term, North Korea tested the Truman Doctrine by invading the Republic of South Korea on June 25, 1950. On June 27 Truman pledged American defense of South Korea and authorized deployment of American troops in Korea without consulting Congress, starting a limited war that would last more than three years. In 1952 Truman declined to run for reelection and retired. Truman supported and advised Lyndon Johnson during the Vietnam War; he died on December 26, 1972.

James Henry Webb Jr.

Born on February 9, 1946, in St. Joseph, Missouri, James Henry Webb Jr. attended the University of Southern California for one year before entering the U.S. Naval Academy. After graduating in 1968, Webb entered the Marine Corps to serve in Vietnam as a company commander, earning the Navy Cross, a Silver Star, two Bronze Stars, the National Achievement Medal, and two Purple Hearts. Before leaving the Marine Corps, he became platoon commander and a member of the secretary of the navy's staff.

After his military service, Webb earned a law degree at Georgetown University in 1975. From 1977 to 1981 he was counsel to the House Committee on Veterans Affairs. He was the first assistant secretary of defense for reserve affairs in the Reagan administration, from 1984 to 1987. In 1987 Webb became secretary of the navy, but he resigned in 1988 to protest congressional budget cuts.

In 1978 Webb won the Horan Award for legal writing and authored his first book, a book about the Vietnam War entitled *Fields of Fire*. Webb has written five best-selling novels, has taught literature at the U.S. Naval Academy, and has won an Emmy Award as a journalist for his coverage of U.S. Marines in Beirut. He also speaks Vietnamese and has done extensive free legal work for the Vietnamese community. He produced and wrote the film *Rules of Engagement*, starring Tommy Lee Jones and Samuel L. Jackson, and he began writing and producing the film version of *Fields of Fire* in 2000.

William Childs Westmoreland

William Childs Westmoreland was born on March 16, 1914, in Spartanburg, South Carolina. He graduated from West Point in

1936. A decorated veteran of World War II and the Korean War, he became the youngest major general in the army at forty-two and the superintendent of West Point at forty-six. In 1964 President Lyndon B. Johnson sent Westmoreland to South Vietnam as deputy commander of the U.S. Military Assistance Command in Vietnam, and within a few months he became commander of all American forces in Vietnam, an office he would hold until 1968.

Although General Westmoreland had no control over most of the air war against North Vietnam, he did direct American operations within South Vietnam. His military strategy was a war of attrition, using search-and-destroy tactics to find and kill Communist soldiers more rapidly than they could be replaced. In February 1968 the Vietminh and the Vietcong launched a combined offensive on Tet, the Vietnamese New Year. Although the Communists suffered major casualties and Westmoreland regarded the outcome as a victory, this display of enemy strength discredited the optimistic reports of the Johnson administration about the progress of the war and demoralized the American people. President Johnson turned toward deescalation and negotiation, replacing Westmoreland with General Creighton Abrams. After Westmoreland returned to Washington to become chief of staff of the army, he complained that Johnson had bullied him into giving news conferences and addresses to Congress to generate support for the war.

As chief of staff from 1968 to 1972, Westmoreland extricated the army from Vietnam and made the transition from the draft to an all-volunteer service during a period of antimilitary sentiment. After retiring, he unsuccessfully sought the Republican nomination for governor of South Carolina in 1974. When the Columbia Broadcasting System accused Westmoreland in a January 1982 television documentary of deceiving President Johnson concerning enemy strength in the Vietnam War, Westmoreland sued CBS for libel, agreeing to an out-of-court settlement in February 1985 and an apology by CBS.

Chronology

1930
February: Ho Chi Minh founds the Indochinese Communist Party to oppose French colonial rule; Le Duan becomes a founding member.

1941
May: Ho Chi Minh returns to Vietnam and establishes the League for Vietnamese Independence, also known as the Vietminh.

1945
September 2: Ho Chi Minh declares Vietnamese independence, establishing the Democratic Republic of Vietnam; Japan signs a treaty surrendering to the Allies.

1946
November 23: French forces attack the Vietnamese harbor of Haiphong, beginning the first Vietnam War between France and the Vietminh.

1947
March 12: President Truman announces the Truman Doctrine, pledging U.S. aid to all free peoples fighting Communist aggression anywhere in the world.

1950
July 26: President Truman authorizes $15 million in military aid to the French forces in Indochina.

1953
September 30: President Eisenhower approves $785 million in military aid to South Vietnam.

1954
April 7: President Eisenhower explains his "domino theory" of foreign policy.

May 7: After the battle of Dien Bien Phu, French forces surrender to the Vietminh and begin withdrawing from Vietnam.

July 21: The Geneva Accords divide Vietnam along the seventeenth parallel, giving Ho Chi Minh's government control of North Vietnam and Bao Dai's government control of South Vietnam and requiring reunification elections in 1956; Bao Dai denounces the agreement and the United States refuses to sign.

September 8: Secretary of State Dulles organizes the Southeast Asia Treaty Organization, an eight-nation coalition pledged to resist Communist aggression in Southeast Asia.

1955
October 26: Ngo Dinh Diem defeats Bao Dai in the South Vietnamese election, establishes the Republic of Vietnam, and becomes the first president; President Eisenhower pledges U.S. support.

1956
July 20: The United States supports Diem's refusal to hold reunification elections.

1959
May: North Vietnam sends military personnel and weapons into South Vietnam; the United States sends military advisers to South Vietnam.

1960
December: South Vietnamese rebels, called Vietcong (Vietnamese Communists) by Diem, form the National Liberation Front.

December 31: U.S. military personnel in Vietnam number nine hundred.

1961
October: President Kennedy authorizes the deployment of more military advisers to South Vietnam and increases financial assistance to the Diem government.

December 31: U.S. military personnel in Vietnam number three thousand two hundred five.

1963

November: Diem is assassinated after a U.S.-supported military coup overthrows his government; Kennedy is assassinated and Lyndon B. Johnson becomes the U.S. president.

December 31: U.S. military personnel in Vietnam number sixteen thousand five hundred.

1964

August 2–4: The USS *Maddox*, an American destroyer, reports being attacked by North Vietnamese patrol boats in the Gulf of Tonkin; the United States retaliates with air strikes on North Vietnam.

August 7: With only two dissenters, Congress passes the Gulf of Tonkin Resolution, giving President Johnson authority to use "all necessary steps, including the use of armed force" in Southeast Asia.

December 31: U.S. military personnel in Vietnam number twenty-three thousand.

1965

February: North Vietnamese forces attack American bases in South Vietnam; President Johnson authorizes Operation Rolling Thunder, a sustained bombing of North Vietnam that continues until October 31, 1968.

March 8: Thirty-five hundred U.S. Marines, the first U.S. combat troops, land in South Vietnam.

March 24: Antiwar teach-ins begin at American universities with the first teach-in at the University of Michigan at Ann Arbor.

April 7: President Johnson offers a $1 billion economic development program for Vietnam if the North Vietnamese will participate in "unconditional discussions"; North Vietnamese prime minister Pham Van Dong rejects the proposal the next day.

April 17: Students for a Democratic Society sponsors the first major antiwar march in Washington, D.C.

October 15–16: Nationwide antiwar demonstrations begin.

December 31: U.S. military personnel in Vietnam number nearly 184,000.

1966

January 28: Senator J. William Fulbright begins hearings of the Senate Foreign Relations Committee to investigate the Vietnam War.

December 31: U.S. military personnel in Vietnam number 385,000.

1967

April 15: More than 100,000 people in New York City and San Francisco demonstrate against the Vietnam War, including civil rights leader Martin Luther King Jr.

October 16–21: Antiwar demonstrations occur nationwide, including a march on the Pentagon in Washington, D.C.

December 31: U.S. military personnel in Vietnam number close to five hundred thousand.

1968

January 30: Communist forces launch the Tet Offensive, a massive surprise attack on South Vietnamese cities during the Vietnamese New Year, which U.S. and South Vietnamese forces repulse after nearly a month of fighting.

March 16: In South Vietnam, Lieutenant William Calley orders his men to fire on the village of My Lai, killing hundreds of unarmed civilians.

March 31: President Johnson suspends the bombing of North Vietnam, invites peace talks with North Vietnam, and announces that he will not run for reelection.

May 13: The United States and North Vietnam begin peace talks in Paris, France.

October 31: President Johnson halts the bombing of North Vietnam, ending Operation Rolling Thunder.

December 31: U.S. military personnel in Vietnam number 540,000.

1969

June 8: President Nixon announces the first withdrawal of 25,000 U.S. troops from Vietnam; U.S. military personnel in Vietnam number 543,000.

October 15: More than 1 million Americans participate in the moratorium antiwar demonstrations nationwide.

November 3: President Nixon requests the support of the "silent majority" for his Vietnamization Plan to gradually withdraw U.S. troops from Vietnam while shifting military responsibilities to South Vietnamese forces.

November 15: The mobilization peace demonstration in Washington, D.C., draws 250,000 people, becoming the largest antiwar protest in U.S. history.

December 31: U.S. military personnel in Vietnam number 479,000.

1970

February 20: National Security Adviser Henry Kissinger begins secret peace talks with North Vietnamese negotiator Le Duc Tho in Paris.

April 29: U.S. and South Vietnamese forces invade Cambodia to attack Communist sanctuaries; major antiwar protests start nationwide.

May 4: Ohio national guardsmen kill four antiwar protesters at Kent State University.

June 24: The U.S. Senate repeals the 1964 Gulf of Tonkin Resolution; U.S. troops withdraw from Cambodia.

December 31: U.S. military personnel in Vietnam number 335,000.

1971

March 29: A military court convicts Lieutenant William Calley of murdering South Vietnamese civilians at My Lai.

April 19–23: The group Vietnam Veterans Against the War demonstrates in Washington, D.C.

June 13: The *New York Times* begins publication of the Pentagon Papers, secret defense documents stolen by Daniel Ellsberg.

December 31: U.S. military personnel in Vietnam number close to 150,000.

1972
March: Communist forces begin the Easter Offensive against South Vietnam.

May 8: President Nixon authorizes the mining of Haiphong Harbor, a naval blockade of North Vietnam, and intensified bombing of North Vietnam.

October: Kissinger and Le Duc Tho reach a cease-fire agreement.

December: When peace talks break down, President Nixon orders the resumption of the bombing of North Vietnam.

December 31: U.S. military personnel in Vietnam number twenty-four thousand.

1973
January 27: The Paris Peace Accords are signed, ending U.S. involvement in the Vietnam War.

March 29: North Vietnam releases the final sixty-seven American prisoners of war and the last U.S. troops leave Vietnam.

December 31: U.S. military personnel in Vietnam number less than 250.

1974
September: President Ford pardons Nixon for any crimes he might have committed as president and offers clemency to draft evaders and military deserters.

1975
April 30: South Vietnam falls to the North Vietnamese as the last Americans leave by helicopter from the roof of the U.S. embassy.

1977
January 21: President Jimmy Carter pardons most of the ten thousand Vietnam War draft evaders on the day after his inauguration.

1978

December: Vietnam invades Cambodia in response to the 1977 Cambodian incursion into Vietnam; thousands of "boat people" flee Vietnam after Vietnamese efforts to nationalize industries and collectivize farms create food shortages.

1979

February 17: China attacks Vietnam to protest Vietnam's invasion of Cambodia but withdraws sixteen days later.

1982

November 11: The Vietnam Veterans Memorial, known as "the Wall," is dedicated in Washington, D.C.

1990

April 30: Vietnamese Communist Party leader Nguyen Van Linh appeals to the United States for friendship and economic cooperation.

1991

April 21: The United States and Vietnam agree to establish a U.S. office in Hanoi to help determine the fate of all soldiers missing in action.

1995

July 11: With bipartisan support in Congress, President Clinton announces the normalization of relations with Vietnam.

1997

May 9: Appointed by President Clinton to be the first postwar U.S. ambassador to Vietnam, Douglas "Pete" Peterson arrives in Hanoi, where he had been a prisoner of war during the Vietnam War.

2000

November 16: President Clinton visits Vietnam.

2001

October 3: The U.S. Senate approves an agreement normalizing trade between the United States and Vietnam.

For Further Research

DAVID L. ANDERSON, ED., *Shadow on the White House: Presidents and the Vietnam War, 1945–1975*. Lawrence: University Press of Kansas, 1993.

————, *Trapped by Success: The Eisenhower Administration and Vietnam, 1953–1961*. New York: Columbia University Press, 1991.

JAMES R. ARNOLD, *The First Domino: Eisenhower, the Military, and America's Intervention in Vietnam*. New York: William & Morrow, 1991.

ANTHONY AUSTIN, *The President's War: The Story of the Gulf of Tonkin Resolution and How the Nation Was Trapped in Vietnam*. Philadelphia: Lippincott, 1971.

LOREN BARITZ, *Backfire: A History of How American Culture Led Us into Vietnam and Made Us Fight the Way We Did*. New York: William & Morrow, 1985.

LAWRENCE M. BASKIR AND WILLIAM A. STRAUSS, *Chance and Circumstance: The Draft, the War, and the Vietnam Generation*. New York: Knopf, 1978.

LARRY BERMAN, *Lyndon Johnson's War*. New York: Norton, 1989.

————, *No Peace, No Honor: Nixon, Kissinger, and Betrayal in Vietnam*. New York: Free Press, 2001.

————, *Planning a Tragedy: The Americanization of the War in Vietnam*. New York: Norton, 1982.

ALEXANDER BLOOM AND WINI BREINES, *"Takin' It to the Streets": A Sixties Reader*. New York: Oxford University Press, 1995.

ROBERT BUZZANCO, *Masters of War: Military Dissent and Politics in the Vietnam Era*. New York: Cambridge University Press, 1996.

JAMES CABLE, *The Geneva Conference of 1954 on Indochina*. New York: St. Martin's, 1986.

NOAM CHOMSKY, *At War with Asia*. New York: Pantheon Books, 1970.

———, *Rethinking Camelot: JFK, the Vietnam War, and U.S. Political Culture*. Boston: South End, 1993.

TAYLOR CLYDE, ED., *Vietnam and Black America: An Anthology of Protest and Resistance*. New York: Anchor, 1973.

CHARLES DEBENEDETTI, *An American Ordeal: The Antiwar Movement of the Vietnam Era*. Syracuse, NY: Syracuse University Press, 1990.

JAMES DICKERSON, *North to Canada: Men and Women Against the Vietnam War*. Westport, CT: Praeger, 1999.

WILLIAM DUDLEY, ED., *The Vietnam War: Opposing Viewpoints*. San Diego: Greenhaven Press, 1998.

LLOYD C. GARDNER, *Pay Any Price: Lyndon Johnson and the Wars for Vietnam*. Chicago: Ivan R. Dee, 1995.

FRED HALSTEAD, *Out Now! A Participant's Account of the American Movement Against the Vietnam War*. New York: Monad, 1978.

GEORGE C. HERRING, *America's Longest War: The United States and Vietnam, 1950–1975*. New York: John Wiley, 1979.

———, *LBJ and Vietnam: A Different Kind of War*. Austin: University of Texas Press, 1994.

———, ED., *American Journey: The Vietnam Era*. Woodbridge, CT: Primary Source Media, 1999.

MICHAEL H. HUNT, *Lyndon Johnson's War: America's Cold War Crusade in Vietnam, 1945–1968*. New York: Hill and Wang, 1996.

HAYNES BONNER JOHNSON AND BERNARD M. GWERTZMAN, *Fulbright, the Dissenter*. New York: Doubleday, 1968.

STANLEY KARNOW, *Vietnam: A History*. New York: Penguin, 1991.

ALEXANDER KENDRICK, *The Wound Within: America in the Vietnam Years, 1945–1974*. Boston: Little, Brown, 1974.

MYRA MACPHERSON, *Long Time Passing: Vietnam and the Haunted Generation*. New York: Doubleday, 1984.

ROBERT MANN, *A Grand Delusion: America's Descent into Vietnam*. New York: Basic Books, 2001.

ALBERT MARRIN, *America and Vietnam: The Elephant and the Tiger*. New York: Viking Penguin, 1992.

JESSICA MITFORD, *The Trial of Dr. Spock, the Rev. William Sloane Coffin Jr., Michael Ferber, Mitchell Goodman, and Marcus Raskin*. New York: Knopf, 1969.

ROBERT W. MULLEN, *Blacks and Vietnam*. Washington, DC: University Press of America, 1981.

LEE RILEY POWELL, *J. William Fulbright and America's Lost Crusade: Fulbright's Opposition to the Vietnam War*. Little Rock: Rose, 1984.

ROBERT D. SCHULZINGER, *A Time for War: The United States and Vietnam, 1941–1975*. New York: Oxford University Press, 1997.

WILLIAM SHAWCROSS, *Side-Show: Kissinger, Nixon, and the Destruction of Cambodia*. New York: Pocket Books, 1979.

MELVIN SMALL, *Covering Dissent: The Media and the Anti-Vietnam War Movement*. New Brunswick, NJ: Rutgers University Press, 1994.

SANDY VOGELGESANG, *The Long Dark Night of the Soul: The American Intellectual Left and the Vietnam War*. New York: Harper and Row, 1974.

TOM WELLS, *The War Within: America's Battle over Vietnam*. Berkeley and Los Angeles: University of California Press, 1994.

RANDALL BENNETT WOODS, *J. William Fulbright, Vietnam, and the Search for a Cold War Foreign Policy*. New York: Cambridge University Press, 1998.

Index